ON ETHNOGRAPHY

Approaches to Language and Literacy Research

(An NCRLL Volume)

Shirley Brice Heath
and
Brian V. Street
with Molly Mills

Teachers College
Columbia University
New York and London

National Conference on Research
in Language and Literacy

Published by Teachers College Press, 1234 Amsterdam Avenue, New York, NY 10027

Published in association with the National Conference on Research in Language and Literacy (NCRLL). For more about NCRLL, see *www.nyu.edu/education/teachlearn/research/ncrll/*

Library of Congress Cataloging-in-Publication Data

Heath, Shirley Brice.
   On ethnography : approaches to language and literacy research / Shirley Brice Heath, Brian V. Street.
      p. cm. — (Approaches to language and literacy research) (Language and literacy series) "An NCRLL volume."
   Includes bibliographical references and index.
   ISBN 978-0-8077-4866-4 (pbk. : alk. paper). — ISBN 978-0-8077-4867-1 (hardcover : alk. paper)
      1. Literacy—Social aspects. 2. Language and culture. 3. Educational anthropology. I. Street, Brian V. II. Title. III. Series.
   LC149.H43   2008
   302.2′244—dc22   2007045833

ISBN 978-0-8077-4866-4 (paper)
ISBN 978-0-8077-4867-1 (hardcover)

Printed on acid-free paper
Manufactured in the United States of America

15   14   13   8 7 6 5 4 3

In memory of
Charles A. Ferguson,
who relished the language details in ethnography,
and
Margaret and Harry Street,
who knew ethnography as "continuous with ordinary life."

Contents

From the NCRLL Editors

Ethnography: As much as we love to read ethnographic tales, many of us feel a bit intimidated by the approach. We worry that we haven't spent enough time, don't have the proper training, or aren't insightful enough to write about culture. In this volume, Shirley Brice Heath and Brian Street invite us into a research conversation, a dialogue that they have been having for many years on studying language, culture, and learning. We gain insight through following the authors' account of how Molly Mills, a novice social scientist, learned to work and think as an ethnographer in an unfamiliar culture—the world of a juggler. The authors share not only how and why they view the world ethnographically, but to what ends—the "what for" of enlightened social policy, including just and equitable language and literacy practices.

We believe that this book, like others in the NCRLL collection, will be useful to a wide range of researchers, including graduate students, novice researchers, and experienced researchers who want to learn about an unfamiliar research tradition or methodology. Heath and Street take us with them as they reflect on entering communities to study language and literacy in the daily lives of people around the world. They teach us ethnographic tools and walk us through decision rules. Drawing on their exceptional body of work in communities, organizations, and institutions across decades and continents, Heath and Street discuss how they formulated research questions, collected and organized field notes and documents, and employed multiple approaches to analyzing their data. They offer advice on writing ethnography, as well as suggestions for further reading. The book is at once scholarly and accessible, authoritative and invitational.

On Ethnography is the fourth volume in the National Conference on Research in Language and Literacy (NCRLL) collection of books published by Teachers College Press. These volumes, written by some of the most prominent researchers in the field, offer insights, information, and guidance in understanding and employing various approaches to researching language and literacy. The first three highly acclaimed books are *On Qualitative Inquiry*, by George Kamberelis and Greg Dimitriadis; *On the Case*, by Anne Haas Dyson and Celia Genishi; and *On Formative and Design Experiments*, by David Reinking and Barbara Bradley. Subsequent books in this collection will include explorations of critically conscious research by Arlette Willis, Helena Hall, Mary Montovan, Catherine Hunter, LaTanya Burke, and Ana Herrera; classroom discourse by David Bloome, Stephanie Power Carter, Beth Morton Christian, Samara Madrid, Sheila Otto, Nora Shuart-Faris, and Mandy Smith; teacher inquiry by Dixie Goswami, Ceci Lewis, Marty Rutherford, and Diane Waff; narrative inquiry by David Schaafsma and Ruth Vinz; and mixed methods by Robert Calfee and Melanie Sperling.

The "On . . ." books: where language and literacy researchers turn to learn. Welcome to the conversation.

—JoBeth Allen and Donna E. Alvermann

Acknowledgments
and an Opening for Conversation

For many years, conversations on language, culture, learning, and ethnography between Brian and Shirley, authors of this volume, have taken place in different parts of the world. We want you as readers to enter this conversation. Debates over the place of ethnographies in language and literacy research will surely continue for some years. This volume brings together our views on both the history and current thrust of deliberations, narratives, and declarations about ethnography as trustworthy social science.

Throughout these chapters, we refer to ourselves by our first names unless we are citing our publications. We do so in the hope that you will engage personally and directly with the dilemmas we all face as scholars who hold high hopes for the continuing advances possible through rigorous work carried out with the help of the ethnographic lens.

We have long planned to write together, and JoBeth Allen and Donna Alvermann have given us the incentive and opportunity to do so. Our thanks go to them and to Carol Collins, formerly of Teachers College Press, for her persistence, loyalty, and balance of optimism and realism about the changing world of publishing. Carole Saltz has been generous and speedy in shepherding this book through the publishing process, and we are grateful to her.

In particular, we thank our editors for their tolerance of our insistence that this volume speak not only to American readers but also to readers of English around the world with keen interests in ethnography. We select international examples, principally from England, the United States, and other countries in which we have each carried out fieldwork (e.g.,

Mexico and Iran) or used ethnographic perspectives (e.g., South Africa, Papua New Guinea, and Nepal). We both have training and field experiences that many readers will not share. Keep this in mind as you read, since it has implications for assumptions we make that may not always match your own. Both of us have worked in languages other than English and in settings where some surrounding languages have never been written. We have logged several hundred thousand air miles in our comparative studies of the uses of language, oral and written. We have both sustained a dogged attention to "literacy" in its many variants across societies and situations. Both of us were among the first to challenge the dichotomous or autonomous view of literacy. By the early 1990s, both of us emphasized visual and performative dimensions that made multimodal literacies critical for understanding social and cognitive dimensions of verbal aspects of written texts. Each of us has studied ways in which scientific understanding and mathematical calculation relate to interpretation and functional uses of symbol systems. We have undertaken these studies in organizations (such as businesses, social service programs, and nongovernmental agencies), settings and situations (such as teashops and employment interviews), and institutions (such as courts, families, and schools).

In our comparative work, we have depended on international colleagues working in diverse, sometimes turbulent, and often underresourced communities. These colleagues opened doors for our research in distant places. Often, these colleagues have been engaged in national and institutional reforms in which choices and functions of different languages in oral and written forms mattered greatly for disenfranchised and marginalized populations. State systems such as those of South Africa, Guatemala, India, Nepal, Papua New Guinea, and Mexico have to think their way forward by selecting among orthographies, dialects, and languages. Policymakers in these locations also must consider legal, educational, and social implications of their language planning decisions. Social justice in matters such as citizenship and equal access to legal counsel, education, and health benefits often hangs precariously on official language choice by governments.

Within the English-dominant worlds of England and the United States, we have both worked in environments where children come to schools from homes that speak one or more languages other than English. We have hoped that our research in these environments could enable educators and policymakers to value the language resources of immigrants and the intergenerational patterns of communication in families and neighborhoods. We have both worked also in entirely English-speaking environments that have undergone wrenching alterations in economic conditions when mines, mills, and manufacturing disappeared and left entire regions without reliable or viable employment.

Archival materials have drawn both of us into deeper understanding of changing patterns of literacy uses across genders and ages. Shirley was instrumental in discovering the first handmade children's library in English and the first short story written for children in English (cf. Heath, 1997a, 2006). These were created by a vicar's wife in Lincolnshire in the early 18th century. Brian has been closely involved with the Mass Observation (MO) Project in the United Kingdom. Begun in the 1930s to document the lives of ordinary people, the MO Project continues to this day with a panel of "observers" with whom Brian has engaged both as trustee of the archive and as a researcher (see Sheridan, Street, & Bloome, 2000). For both of us, the social history of literacy in the daily lives of communities around the world continues to be a critical part of any study of contemporary policies, practices, and ideologies of language.

Both of us have also worked intensively with national change programs related to literacy, mathematics, and creative learning. We have engaged with policymakers at both local and international levels in ways that have been instructive about policymaking and educational practice. Shirley has worked in England with Creative Partnerships, a government-sponsored effort that began in 2001 to promote creative learning in the arts and sciences within underresourced schools and communities. Brian has contributed to the Global Monitoring Report on Literacy produced by UNESCO and disseminated to agencies developing literacy policies for the first decades of the 21st century. As president of the British Association for Literacy in Development (BALID), he has been engaged in efforts by Civil Society Organizations (CSOs) in the United Kingdom to keep up the momentum on literacy development around the world.

Through the many kinds of work each of us does in literacy research, policy, and practice, we benefit from the wisdom and experience of colleagues in the United Kingdom, the United States, and around the world. With some of these, such as Dave Baker, David Barton, Jan Blommaert, David Bloome, Courtney Cazden, Eve Gregory, Dorothy Holland, Nancy Hornberger, Mary Hamilton, Gunther Kress, Jean Lave, Constant Leung, Susan Lytle, Ben Rampton, Alan Rogers, Dorothy Sheridan, Morag Styles, Jennifer Wolf, and Shelby Wolf, among others, we enjoy the kind of creative dialogue we hope will take place more widely through the pages of this book. Our students and co-ethnographers will see themselves and hear their voices in these pages. We want them to know how much we have gained from our work with them and from the advances they have made in the academic and policy worlds.

The insights that have come from all our inside and outside encounters have informed our thinking about ethnography, language, and literacy. We hope these have helped us translate our experiences in ways that will benefit readers ready to engage with language and literacy research through ethnography.

CHAPTER 1

Language, Culture, and Learning: Ethnographic Approaches

> Humans, more than any other species, spend their time producing symbolic structure for one another. We are very good at coordinating with the regularities in the patterns of symbolic structure that we present to one another. (Hutchins, 1995, p. 370)

Roger is a young man who juggles. He juggles for fun, relaxation, and challenge. He entertains his family and friends. Strangers walking along the street stop to watch him and ask how he learned to juggle. Roger does not mind talking about how he learned to juggle and what juggling means to him. He even talks to ethnographers who are curious about how individuals voluntarily take on complex learning challenges. Molly Mills is such an ethnographer.[1] When she asks Roger about how he started as a juggler, he muses:

> "Actually, when I started learning to juggle, I was just taught by a friend in the very beginning. It was very much like book-learning: It was almost as if you had taken a class. I could always juggle two balls in one hand like that [Roger demonstrates] because there is no pattern to it. It's just immediately obvious."

> "I was in the 6th grade, and I'd just practice constantly, because I just thought it was the coolest thing ever."

> "I think [I] soon learned, just by trial and error, that if [I] threw it up higher, [I] would have more time to catch the ball, which would be easier, but [my] throws would be a little less accurate."

"It's all about practice, trial and error; [I've] got to see what stuff worked and what didn't and then muscle memory."

"After maybe an hour, I could get on it well, standing with a wall next to me."

"I'd remember jugglers I'd seen; I'd see jugglers on TV or something; then I'd try to emulate the really easy patterns."

"[I] knew what it felt like, and [I'd] try to emulate that again."

When we as ethnographers study language and literacy, we are a lot like Roger.

We think it's cool, we read books, we find ways to practice. And we have to admit to the power of trial and error, focus on remembering how others learn to be ethnographers, and try out patterns we hope we can emulate.

Molly Mills is an ethnographer who did all this. She found out that anyone who wants to learn to juggle has to do all that Roger does. She also found out that ethnographers who study language, culture, and learning face special difficulties. They have to figure out how human beings "coordinate with the regularities in the patterns of symbolic structure" in some of the same ways that Roger learns juggling.

Throughout this volume, as we talk about ethnography in the study of language and literacy, we often return to metaphors that surround juggling. We see learning ethnography as being a lot like learning to juggle. Both call for practice, close observation, and the challenge of having to manage more and more balls in the air. Both involve figuring out and hanging onto definitions, principles of operation, and motivational incentives. Both are about constant learning. Both depend on observing, comparing, reflecting, assessing, and coming to "feel" certain stages of achievement in knowledge and skill that do not easily translate into words. Both make use of various means and modes in different combinations at various stages of learning. Finally, both engage learners in figuring out many multiples that go beyond any single moment of insight, step toward expertise, or sense of disappointment.

Here, in place of a perhaps expected definition of ethnography, we jump right into what ethnographers who read this book will have as their central research focus—language and multimodal literacies. We go then first to the object rather than to the method of study, because we believe that we all have to know that we want to learn before someone else tells us how to learn. Furthermore, as you will see, our view of ethnography becomes increasingly evident and even definable as chapters of this book unfold. In the end, you will determine your own. But if you are someone who wants methods first and theoretical distinctions later, then skip Chapter 1 for now, go directly to Chapters 2 through 5, and then read Chapters 1 and 6.

Figuring out what language, culture, and learning can be for ethnographers takes us head-first into *culture*.[2] As we study how humans go about producing "symbolic structure for one another," we see immense variability as well as stability in the ways they create, sustain, and adapt their modalities, including oral and written language. In this volume, we consider only three of the many situations of learning that ethnographers studying language and literacy enter:

1. Individuals striving to become expert in something
2. Groups in identity-making
3. Institutions of formal education

As we travel through illustrations of these three contextual frames, we do need definitions, and we will provide them. We start with some of the conceptual balls that ethnographers who do research on language and multimodal literacies have to juggle.

LANGUAGES AND LITERACIES IN SYMBOLIC STRUCTURE

We take the term *language* to mean any symbol system whose grammar provides phonological, morphological, syntactic, and lexical structures and rules. *Grammar* for linguists amounts to the large-scale system of patterning of units of sound, categories of meaning (e.g., plurality, gender, etc.), and arrangements of units of meaning (e.g., prefixes, suffixes, and roots) that constitute spoken language. Only a fraction of the 6,900 or so languages spoken in the world have writing systems, and few of these appear in a significant amount of printed material (see http://www.ethnologue.com/ethno_docs/distribution.asp?by=country [accessed December 19, 2007]).

Though the word *literacies* shows up everywhere today, we use the simple singular term *literacy* to refer only to written representations of oral (or gestural) language rendered in some script system that carries its own conventions and rules of usage.

In contrast, when we use the term *multimodal literacies*, we mean systems of representation that include written forms that are combined with oral, visual, or gestural modes. Think, for example, of musical scores, choreographic notational systems, computer programming languages, or the script with director's notes for a dramatic performance in American or British Sign Language.

We also recognize *multimodalities*, such as the stance and hand signals of traffic police that drivers "read" and act upon accordingly. Written language has no saliency in this event at this moment, though during their training, police learn from materials in which visual illustrations appear along with printed text.

This is a good place to introduce yet another definitional distinction we use—that between *organizations* and *institutions*. The former appear and disappear, primarily to meet contemporary and often short-lived specialized needs of societies. Though regulated by governmental systems in some cases, organizations have no official State function. Organizations include entities as varied as Girl Scouts and Boy Scouts, corporations, self-help groups, artists' cooperatives, and trade guilds. Institutions, on the other hand, persist, and much of their effort goes into sustaining themselves to meet the lasting needs of their societies. Their functions and purposes do not go away. Governments or state systems, religions, families, formal education systems, and judicial systems affect the lives of all human beings. Though dissent, fragmentation, and dissolution of one kind or another take place within institutions, they remain. Ethnographers benefit from awareness of the origins and purposes of institutions and organizations before they start to probe the consequent differences in their means of sustaining themselves. For example, many community youth groups as organizations have freedoms of time, space, activity, and authority that schools as institutions seldom provide. To do so could alter their fundamental norms of standardization necessary to assure society of their predictability into perpetuity.

Today's scholars who do their research in nations with one dominant national language have to keep in mind not only multimodal literacies but also *multiple languages.* In most nations of the world, learning at least two, and often several, languages before the age of 5 is the norm. From award-winning motion pictures to multinational business call centers, the contemporary world reflects *multilingualism.* Speakers of several languages often have different levels of competency and comfort in reading and writing the languages they speak and understand. For example, children in South African villages often understand and speak as many as five languages before they go to school; when they enter school, they usually learn to read and write in only two of these—English plus the dominant regional language. Today, leaders of the European Union must speak (at least) three languages, though they may not read and write all three with equal ease. Seeing multilingualism as the norm is common among political, educational, and business leaders in India, Indonesia, and many nations of Africa and the Pacific. Multilingualism is likely to be a daily reality in the lives of students around the world, making this phenomenon increasingly significant for definitions and methods used in the teaching of English language and literature around the world (cf. Ellis, Fox, & Street, 2007).

Added to the multiples of languages and literacies that ethnographers encounter in any single setting is the challenge of recording how these work hand in hand with cultural patterns. From pronouncing vowels to shaping stories, every speaker reflects habits, loyalties, and ideologies of language forged in cultural patterns that existed before they were born. From the moment an infant emerges from the womb until death, these cultural patterns, shifting and cumulative as they are, provide the bases through which every human creates, explores, sustains, and tests social relationships while developing a sense of agency.

Talking, gesturing, and waving artifacts about in locally acceptable patterns make up the glue for conversation in all human groups. But these patterns vary across languages and societies, and they change also for individuals as they mature and gain experience with different audiences, settings, and purposes. Institutions and organizations develop their own norms and genres of interactive oral and written exchange, and success in adopting these can mean the difference between membership and exclusion for individuals. The cultural patterning of interaction shapes identities and roles that then provide access and opportunities for learners. From individuals to institutions, shifts in these patterns mean constant learning. Entire fields of study, such as organizational learning or school reform, as well as more familiar fields such as human development, look at language as central to adaptive learning across the individual life span as well as within organizational and institutional trajectories.

Ethnographers face perhaps their greatest challenge as they try to understand how cultural patterns support, deny, and change structures and uses of language and multimodal literacies. Perhaps no anthropologist or educator has done more to point out the importance of this challenge than Dell Hymes. The originator of the idea of *ethnography of communication,* Hymes provided leadership through his own long-term fieldwork among Native Americans of the Northwest as well as his provocative writings on the embeddedness of language in ideology, socialization, and identity (Hymes, 1962, 1964a, 1964b, 1974, 1994, 1996). Hymes and others in linguistic anthropology (see Duranti, 2001, for an overview of this work) demonstrate that bringing ethnography to symbol structuring means not only describing what is currently happening at the local level but also documenting how organizational and institutional forces select and shape their preferred cultural patterns and imbue them with particular values (Leung, 2005).

CULTURE AS A VERB

Anthropologists have long debated the meaning of the term *culture*. By the end of the 20th century, many had pointed out the neocolonial, racist, and nationalist overtones of the term. (See Chapter 6 for the history of ethnography leading up to the era of post-colonial studies.) Meanwhile, scholars from other fields (e.g., business, medicine, and sports) adopted the term "culture," taking it to be almost synonymous with "ambience," "climate," or "spirit." Social constructivists and some anthropologists (including Brian and Shirley) pushed hard for the idea that culture never just "is," but instead "does" (Thornton, 1988, p. 26). Street (1993b) proposed that we think of culture as a verb rather than as a noun—a fixed thing. Ethnographers who adopted this idea took culture to be unbounded, kaleidoscopic, and dynamic.

In their studies of ever-shifting active processes of meaning-making in situations, ethnographers search for interconnected patterns (see Shuman, 1986, for an illustration of this principle in a study of secondary students in and out of school). In their focused observation and participation within a chosen physical location or an identifiable social group, ethnographers adopting the culture-as-verb idea take as axiomatic the following principles as they think ahead to their field studies of language and multimodal literacies.

1. Gradations of change in habits and beliefs (though seemingly minor on the surface) correlate with shifts in structures and uses of language and multimodal literacies.
2. Singular or "essential" meanings or explanations that come in authoritative or institutionally grounded terms must be open to scrutiny in historical and operational frames.
3. The same goes for discourse forms and illustrative materials that stick out or are formalized, authorized, named, and valorized (especially through state-sanctioned and -supported institutions or commercial interests).
4. Insiders or locals use tacit meaning-making processes that they take for granted, and their explanations of these often bear little relationship to realities of usage. They may be expressing *ideals* of behavior rather than *manifest*, or actual, behavior.
5. The norm in (almost) all contexts is that we coordinate the regularities of patterns of several systems of symbolic structure at the same time.

Already you see that the complexities of this kind of juggling will not be easy. It is heavily conceptual, requires accuracy, and begs for models to emulate.

Widespread public usage of the nouns "a culture" or "cultures" makes the ethnographer's work especially difficult. Nouns such as these lead people to believe in fixed boundaries around things and events as well as beliefs and values. Phrases or terms such as "my culture," as distinct from "your culture," or cultures subsumed within the term "multicultural," accentuate differences and borders.

The fact is that the work of ethnographers shows again and again that groups that see themselves as vastly different from their neighboring groups actually share many habits and patterns of behavior. Yet the *meta-narratives* or stories they tell in order to give reasons for their particular history or cultural patterns may differ greatly. Meta-narratives answer questions that ask "why do we do this and not that?" Groups use these stories (many of which show up in literature, rhymes, and lullabies for children) to keep up the idea of their own unique identity.

We generally associate "culture" with one or more "societies," often seen as synonymous with "nation," "racial group," "religion," or "ethnicity." Yet these biological and geographic frames of birth origin or chosen affinity also develop sub-groupings that have a strong sense of their own special ways of doing and believing. For example, members of every nation, though held together within national boundaries, will vary along a spectrum of differences that result from their history of migration, group isolation, geographic locale, religious affiliation, and other internal or external forces. Think, for example, of the vast differences of language and social grouping reflected in contemporary Mexico, Canada, South Africa, Indonesia, or the Philippines. Racial labeling changes not only under different governments but also from evolving preferences for self-naming by the groups themselves. Think of the changing history of power within labels such as *Negro, African, African American* (with and without a hyphen), *Black,* or *Afro-Caribbean,* and the role that individuals identified by these labels played in bringing particular terms to public acceptance and usage.

Institutions as well as organizations that carry no inherent ties to place of origin also develop core cultural patterns and meta-narratives about their "culture." Institutions of formal education pride themselves on their particular "culture" and use their distinctiveness in promotion and recruitment.

Organizations do the same. Consider, for example, portrayals of "the Hewlett Packard way" on the pages of business magazines at the end of the 20th century or the notion that certain sports (never mind particular teams, such as the Boston Red Sox, Manchester United, or Real Madrid) develop identifiable "cultures." In popular uses of the term "culture," the underlying generally unspecified referent is a core of complexly intertwined symbols, habits, and beliefs generally selected not on a descriptive basis but as prescriptive norms. Corporate groups, sports teams, and other organizations consciously build and promote their own "culture" for public relations purposes. Insiders or old-timers often judge newcomers by the extent to which they adopt certain key values or behaviors identified with "our culture." Failure to act as a member in "good" cultural standing can, and often does, lead to ostracism or expulsion. The notion of "communities of practice" attempts to build on these ideas, especially in the context of business enterprise (Wenger, 1998; but cf. Barton and Tusting, 2005, for a perspective more in tune with the account we provide here of cultural processes and their relation to language and power).

Complexes of cultural habits and beliefs change for institutions and organizations as well as social groups. Some of these changes take place in the open while others go on behind the scenes or without participants' awareness. Stimulating such changes in almost every circumstance are pressures and forces— social, political, and economic—from outside the group. Powerful individual personalities can also shift the sense of cultural identity or potential of such groups.

Ethnographers face loose and varying popularized definitions of "culture" in every setting. As they sort out and describe what actually happens as well as what locals and outsiders believe is happening or happened in the past, they keep culture as a verb. Narratives, logos, slogans, and codified sets of instructions, as well as written histories and accounts by outsiders or dissidents, together help reveal the web of meanings that build and shift as people use language and multimodal literacies.

Learning Across Recurring Situations

Historically, studies that take *culture* as a noun also take language to be both model and vehicle of cultural processes that surround learning. As model, language is taken as our primary representation of cultural knowledge. As vehicle, language is considered the means by which we transmit what we know and think. Neither conveys the integrative complexities of language in interplay with culture and, most especially, with our ways of knowing and learning.

As ethnographers come to understand culture as a verb, they recognize that the vast majority of what and how humans learn never goes into language as either model or vehicle. Think of the play of infants and toddlers, for example. Speakers and users of language and multimodal literacies generally find it difficult to think analytically about what they know and do. Much that we learn as members of our different cultural entities will not fit easily into any set of symbols, no matter how complex the arrangement. Knowledge that comes in patterned symbolic structure works in constant interdependence with context, emotion, embodiment, and many other aspects of being human. Sorting out as many connections of language and culture as possible across recurring and definable situations constitutes the ethnographer's job.

To illustrate such connections, we lay out three situations that come up again and again across the life span. These represent only a small selection of the slices of life in which ethnographers can locate their studies of learning, but they are selected as particularly appropriate for those adopting an ethnographic perspective on language and literacy. We look at individuals setting their own goals toward expertise; groups building their identities; and formal education institutions transmitting prescribed values, skills, and bodies of information.

As humans mature biologically and neurologically, everyday behaviors (such as walking) take place without representation by symbol systems. But actions and communications that reflect meaning recur throughout the course of life and lend themselves to study through the primary tools of collecting and analyzing data that ethnographers use.

Individuals in Expertise Achievement

The first of these recurring situations involves individuals who set out to become expert in one particular area of achievement. We focus on situations in which individuals voluntarily work toward getting better at one or another complex set of skills. Like Roger the juggler, they learn by observing, experimenting, practicing, and self-assessing; they may also seek direct instruction. A young person wants to learn to unicycle. A gamer wants to improve skills in an occasional after-work pastime. A retiree takes up woodworking and becomes expert in making a special design of salad bowl. Individuals who voluntarily pursue special roles or forms of expertise use "practical intelligence." Psychologist Robert Sternberg and colleagues study managers and others who work in "practical" fields that call for "everyday problem-solving skills." They describe ways that "practical intelligence" differs from "academic" intelligence (Sternberg, 1985; Sternberg & Wagner, 1986, 1994. See also Rose, 2004, on the expertise of waitresses and other keen strategists). Though debates rage about different kinds of "intelligence," most scholars agree that identity as a successful individual in chosen pursuits rests solidly on: (1) observation and purposeful seeking out of experts as sources (through apprenticeship, lectures, readings, or video materials); (2) creation of one's own strategies in problem solving; and (3) persistence in self-assessment and goal-setting. (Sometimes, but by no means in the majority of cases, expertise also includes verbal explanation of just how to become or to work as an expert with a certain skill or knowledge subset.)

The scientist and philosopher Michael Polanyi (1966/1983) called these particular combinations of ways of knowing *tacit knowledge*—both unconscious and inexpressible. Though this term has been applied to many everyday behaviors, Polanyi himself focused on certain kinds of achievement, such as bicycling or juggling. Every cyclist and juggler talks about what he or she does, how the skills came about, and how they are practiced and altered. But full explanations in mathematical, cognitive, or even social terms can never explain what is "really" learned. Experts often sum up their process of achievement by advising: "Just do it, enjoy it, and be willing to work at it."

But mastering expertise takes more than any verbal explanation can capture. Patterns develop deep in our muscles and memory. Serious practice, deep thinking, and mental imaging help us remember and build from actions and interactions that seem to be "in" our bodies. Finger-tapping on a desk by a pianist is not embodied in quite the same way as the impatient tapping of a customer at a service desk. Much that we learn is embodied learning (Dourish, 2001; Pfeifer & Bongard, 2007). Roger the juggler refers to this as "muscle memory."

Molly, the ethnographer who studied Roger, wanted to describe and analyze the behaviors that came together around his self-conscious expertise. She observed his actions and listened to how his talk reflected "regularities in the patterns of symbolic structure that we present to one another" (Hutchins, 1995, p. 370). She wanted to understand how Roger's uses of verbal language and other modalities related to how he learned his skills and sense of identity as a juggler.

Groups in Identity-Making

Ethnographers who study groups who make and sustain their identities draw on methods that go beyond those Molly used to study Roger as an individual working to achieve expertise. A prime example of a group comes from anthropologist Edwin Hutchins (1995) in his studies of ship navigation in the San Diego harbor. (For a similar study, carried out much earlier in the South Seas, see Gladwin, 1970, who studied the natives of Puluwat who sail canoes without instruments over expanses of the Pacific Ocean.) Hutchins analyzes individual introspection; the distribution among members of the group of formal manipulations of numbers, symbols, and lines on charts; and on-the-spot communication as well as later reflections by participants. He looks at how paths of learning work together as the seamen navigate ships into harbor, often under unpredictable traffic and weather conditions. Only with group coordination of the distributed intelligence of these navigators and ship captains and crew can ships enter the harbor safely.

Hutchins (1995) goes beyond the individual to capture the adaptive and ongoing learning behind and within the "everyday" maneuvers of ship crews and navigators. He lets us in on what the term "expert system" means. Certainly, much expertise lies in the artifacts, but what actually happens results from "the system of person-in-interaction-with-technology." He reminds us that "tools permit the people using them to do the tasks that need to be done while doing the kinds of things that people are good at: recognizing patterns, modeling simple dynamics of the world, and manipulating objects in the environment" (p. 155).

Every ethnographer who sets out to study one or more groups works in the shadow of earlier representations of similar groups or situations. We sense these shadows most when we study groups, such as cultural communities, organizations, and sports teams, whose public identities carry social, political, and economic weight. Even within these groups, members recall and present themselves through selective and ever-changing memories. Identities shift as group members both sustain old habits and values and invent new ways to relate, display, and transmit who they are and how they came to be as well as what they see themselves becoming.

Members see themselves as "belonging" to a group with definable characteristics they refer to as "our culture." Members sustain themselves through learning to be and to work together, knowing that their representation to the outside world depends on how effectively they create and maintain their identity. As noted earlier, much of this "public culture" may be prescriptive, while the ethnographer's job is descriptive and analytical. As entities, limited spatially, by affinity, or through self-assigned membership, these groups may include villages or neighborhoods or even large closely knit families and community organizations—what Holland, Skinner, Lachiotte, and Cain (1998) refer to as "figured worlds."

As noted earlier, individuals, institutions, organizations and social groupings (such as villages or small towns) can purposefully attempt to alter their public representation of themselves even when internal values and behaviors may not have changed in significant ways. Consider, for example, multinational oil companies that have been involved in widely reported oil spills. In the 1990s, advertisements of several of these companies shifted away from pictures of cars and airplanes or oil rigs and graphs and charts of company achievements and profits. Instead, advertisements in magazines carried a single photograph of a dove in flight plus printed text telling a story about the value of nature's symbols for reminding us of the beauty of the earth. Readers had to consciously search to locate the name of the oil company in tiny print at the bottom of the page. This seemingly small change was followed within a decade by the inclusion in magazines of advertising sections that represent themselves as "news," "human interest stories," or "environmental moral tales." Through these changes of self-representation, corporations try to shed their "black" image for a "green" one.

We need to look closely and think consciously to distinguish group-identity advertisements from news or feature articles that report on actions by these groups. As corporate identities insert themselves more and more "ordinarily" into everyday scenes, the public (sometimes helped by ethnographers; see Chapter 6) needs to attend not only to what these advertisers portray as their group "cultures" but also to what their groups actually do and value.

An additional issue that often draws ethnographers' attention is the matter of how groups change over time without recognizing that they do so. As noted earlier, the dynamism of cultural lives comes, more often than not, primarily through nearly imperceptible shifts in actions, collective memories, and signs and systems of symbols.

How we draw in the sand, signal distress, or sense the way the wind is blowing depends on collections of signs that make meanings that surpass, supplement, and even contradict what may be reported by insiders as unchanged and unchanging. For example, in the central desert of Australia, telling stories while drawing in the sand is an age-old cultural practice (Eickelkamp, 1999; Kral, 2007). Stories in this context have long centered on ancient tales, hunting and gathering practices, and family and land connections. In the past three decades, rapid and far-reaching disruptions of these traditional patterns have come with settlement of kin groups into communities dependent on public monies. Today elders rarely create these stories, and the stories that children illustrate in the sand tell of contemporary interpersonal stress and family tensions.

Yet elders report that the old sand-stories are still alive, but children "know different," for their sense of what is "alive" is not the same as that of their parents and grandparents. In other words, the elders see the children as continuing the ancient practice of storytelling and sand-drawing and therefore believe "the tradition" remains. Yet the substance and message of the practice have changed as well as the primary practitioners, as Kral (2007) demonstrates in her accounts of how Aboriginal children use new media technologies to tell their stories. Within every group, ethnographers and close observers find contradictions between what is believed and expressed and what is actually done and is often inexpressible. Ethnographers have to recognize and document both.

Institutions of Formal Education

From sites of formal schooling, ethnographers most often choose classrooms as their entity of focus. Here learners come together not by self-chosen expertise goals or small-group identity but by external assignment. Direct instruction by a designated expert comes primarily through oral language with substantial reinforcement from specialized artifacts, such as textbooks, worksheets, whiteboards, and tests. Ethnographers who study classrooms note the range of symbol systems that support and often define specific zones of time and place, such as literacy hour or reading circle. Ethnographers capture instructor-sanctioned events of students as well as moments when learners play out their self-assigned roles, such as bully, class clown, or geek. Ethnographers attend also to the nonmembers who come and go in classrooms (parents, students from other classrooms, and volunteers). The manner and content of how these outsiders get introduced, take part, and present themselves matter to ethnographers (Bloome, Carter, Christian, Otto, & Shuart-Faris, 2005).

Since the 1990s, classrooms have become the most frequently researched site of ethnographers. Yet classrooms, like all sanctioned sites of formal education, receive their identities, spaces, times, and instructional goals primarily from power sources beyond local participants. Pace, methods, and artifacts for display of skills and information, as well as standards of achievement (rarely referred to as "expertise"), derive from core parameters of formal education (e.g., time, space, and role specifications).

We consider here ways that historical and political forces behind these parameters determine language, modalities, and norms of use for institutions of formal education. It is these to which the ethnographer must attend, not just the immediate "face-to-face" observables. These external impositions dictate means and levels of learning. Formal education systems in all societies are tightly bound to either religion or the state or, in some cases, to both. Institutions of religion and government depend on permanent written records of their authority and achievements. Archival records and sacred texts of state and religious powers lie behind control of daily activities and transmission of belief systems. Consider the Magna Carta, the Declaration of Independence, the Constitution of Australia, the Quoran, and the Bible.

A bit of history helps here. When formal education systems came into being as instruments of government, sanctioned and preferred ways of using written language came along with explicit instruction of bodies of knowledge.[3] Whether simply for receptive use (such as reading and reciting only) or in productive functions (such as writing and illustrating through elaboration of certain elements of a script), written language evolved at a rapid pace, becoming the ultimate tool of power for formal education systems linked to the state. Yet until the beginning of the 18th century in Europe, even within higher education institutions, oratory, oral deliberation, and dramatic performance also carried considerable power. People identified political and religious leaders by their oral skills (Vincent, 1989).

Nevertheless, by the end of the 18th century, literacy had taken hold across much of North America, as well as in England, and perhaps to a lesser extent in Europe (Olson, 1977). Formal education systems now looked to reading and writing as key marks of individual power and status. Even leisure time came to be linked with the ability to read. Public libraries, newspaper distribution, and publication of fiction and poetry spread rapidly. Conversation manuals often promoted reading in leisure time to stimulate verbal depth and dexterity. During this period, museums also began to capture those members of society who had leisure time, and every visit fed curiosity about distant places as well as awareness of contemporary breakthroughs in cartography and botanical and anatomical illustration. Print became ubiquitous. Notions of "standard," "official," or "state languages" evolved in close association with the importance of formal education and achievement by individuals of the status of "literate."

This brief history tells us a great deal about the underlying valuations of written languages. Individuals who cannot use the "official" languages or standard varieties of their countries or write that language in "standard" form have beliefs about language and literacy that affect their perceptions of themselves. Therefore, even when the arm of formal education has not directly reached such individuals, the influence of the authoritative status that formal schooling gives written language or a particular "standard" form of language extends far into and deep within a nation.

Moreover, chosen uses and forms of language have through the past two centuries increasingly become synonymous with learning and achievement in general. An individual is considered "learned" or well educated if he or she speaks a particular form of language, can read and write the correlate of that form according to prescribed conventions, and knows how to use particular oral and written language forms together to wield power. In addition, one's language uses portray a breadth of sanctioned experiences that can add up to being labeled "cosmopolitan," "a citizen of the world," or "well rounded."

What are the implications of all of this for ethnography? Rigorous research distinguishes linguistic or literate skills and knowledge associated with institutions of formal education from processes of learning that individuals and groups develop in their own expertise and identity-making. The latter kinds of learning can be interdependent with school-sanctioned language and modes, but often individual and group expertise passes unnoted and unvalued. This is especially the case for wisdom and experience valued in cultural communities easily pushed to the side in favor of "advanced" technologies. Consider, for example, the long-standing botanical/medical knowledge local healers of rural areas and indigenous groups hold in various parts of the world.

Formal education, viewed as a unified program of change planned and organized by the norms and ideologies of groups in power, opens endless opportunities for ethnographers to ask about how learning is displayed and valued in relation to different combinations of multimodalities. We note below a few starting points for looking deep inside language, literacy, and multimodalities in classrooms. In each case, we note the need to set spatial and temporal boundaries when seeking the answer to questions.

Ethnographers can examine learning across language, literacy, and multimodalities in myriad ways, including the following:

1. *Describe and contrast student and teacher talk about textbook content.*

   Possible key questions: To what extent do teachers and students balance their talk about information gained from printed texts as distinct from other illustrative materials? How do assessments of students reflect a balance, and which patterns of language structures and uses receive the most positive valuations of student knowledge of textbook content?

2. *Describe and contrast classroom language in a related subject area (e.g., English, science, etc.) with the interactive talk of adults and*

young learners preparing for an event such as a school drama or community recycling campaign.

Possible key questions: What will speakers' vocabulary, syntax, genres, reference points, and interruptions of one another look like in these contrastive situations? How do participants themselves describe any differences they see in their language uses in classrooms and in after-school organized activities? What do they believe influences these differences?

3. *Describe and contrast ways in which primary teachers call upon representational schema to teach pupils about time, space, and so on.*

Possible key questions: What are the differences between digital and analog representations of time (e.g., 24-hour digital clocks/12-hour circular clock faces)? What are the "affordances" of each type? How do school practices relate to those that pupils are familiar with in their everyday lives (e.g., video recording or bus timetable layouts that use different representations of time)?

Signs and symbols are not "innocent" (cf. Bourdieu, 1991; Bourdieu & Passeron, 1977). A broad effort for ethnographers of classrooms should go to identifying conventions that students learn that parallel (and often originate from) those of "real" life. Consider, for example, conventions surrounding plagiarism and legal constraints behind the need to credit sources within textbooks and documentary films. Textbook publishers cannot simply take an illustration or photograph from another source without securing and citing permission. Documentary filmmakers cannot, without permission, lift portions of graphs or charts from newspapers or sections of earlier films or even "amateur" digital recordings without facing legal repercussions. Every ethnographer studying the production, reception, and uses of these multimodal literacies sees in these artifacts the representation of the prohibition against plagiarism. Students are admonished not to plagiarize, but they rarely understand this warning in the context of the legal issues that publishers and filmmakers face.

In essence, every student, textbook writer, and filmmaker is expected to learn certain conventions of attribution to ensure "credit" for direct copying. Students who do "research papers" must learn the conventions of punctuating quotations, footnoting, citing references, and offering acknowledgments. All conventions, many far less obvious than those noted here, lend themselves to scrutiny by ethnographers who want to understand hidden and overt expectations in the "culture" of classrooms. Many conventions and norms find representation primarily through admonition against unsanctioned practices rather than through sustained explication and consideration in terms of their origins or comparative contexts and purposes.

Educational systems in particular (and Western societies more broadly) are often criticized for overemphasizing the significance of writing and speech as the central salient modes of representation (Kress & Van Leeuwen, 2001). Yet artifacts within schools and other formal institutions and organizations depend on illustrations of a wide variety of types. We turn now to multimodalities and ways to define and identify these even in the midst of dominant language and literacy forms in schools.

MULTIMODALITIES

A primary job of ethnographers is to track, describe, and enumerate multimodalities as *semiotic* resources in their combinations—linguistic, gestural, kinesthetic, and visual (Kress & Van Leeuwen, 1996, 2001). Modes, socially learned and displayed, support individuals, groups, and institutions as they gain and sustain expertise and identity (e.g., as computer geek or graffiti artist; as dance troupe or football team; as kindergarten or business school). When ethnographers study any of the three situations of life-span learning noted above, they see systems of arrangement not only within each mode but in ways modes work together.

We use the term *multimodal literacies* to refer to those events and practices in which the written mode is still salient, yet embedded in other modes. These can initially be observed most readily within situations in which some agent, organization, or institution wants to transmit information, build skills, change attitudes, entertain, or accomplish all of these goals at the same time.

Think, for example, of contemporary "classic" comic books, narrative television advertisements, or a magazine such as *Adbuster* (published in Canada). This magazine plays off inside knowledge of the advertising and marketing worlds to show what is happening in the "mental environment" of consumers. A variety of modes are called upon to do this work, written modes being embedded in such features of visual mode as color, layout, and so on. Usual conventions or genres (such as advertisement, editorial, or exposition) of printed texts are not immediately obvious to first-time readers of this magazine. Each new reader of *Adbuster* has to learn how to read against conventions of prior expectations in order to figure out the parodic intent of the subtext of the magazine. Back cover and front cover look "alike" in gross format, but the two generally contradict each other. The front cover announces the "culture of life" while the back cover proclaims the "culture of death." The magazine is printed right side up for one-half of the inside text pages and in reverse for the other half. Several languages cut in and out of the pages in every issue. Close scrutiny of almost any page reveals that what seems familiar is strange.

Though not so ideologically "out front" as *Adbuster,* science textbooks in formal education systems carry similar instances in which texts and images cross-reference other sources of information, such as scientific report, newspaper, recipe book, or pamphlet from the family dentist (cf. Jewitt, 2006). In science textbooks, written language comes along with graphs, charts, schematic drawings, and photographs. These work together in (sometimes) systematic ways within sections of textbooks and across textbooks as a whole. In many cases, certain patterns of arrangements of the multiple modes used within any single text are echoed in other volumes in a series. For example, laboratory manuals pick up patterns used in accompanying textbooks and also represent actual hands-on work through diagrams and step-by-step illustrations.

Consider another detail that matters in terms of presuppositions that teachers, textbook makers, and test developers make about students' uses of printed text and illustrations. Think here especially of the difficulties that non-native speakers face in reading a science textbook in a classroom full of unfamiliar and unexplained conventions. In science textbooks, captions that accompany illustrations only sometimes relate to the written text. Some echo the fuller printed text with synonyms, while some explode into analogical comparison. Some illustrations "count" as carrying information to be remembered or to note as exemplary of points made in the written text. Other illustrations may only be fillers to "lighten" the weight of the detailed material presented in print. A biology textbook may on the same double-page spread include schematic drawings labeled "Figure 10a, 10b," and so on, with reference to these figures within the printed text. Yet on the same page, a photograph may appear with no caption or text reference. Readers are somehow expected to figure out on their own the relevance of visual materials to the broader arguments of the printed text. Presuppositions about learners' abilities to "see" connections and to add meaning underlie ways that producers of multimodal materials combine these resources (cf. Kress & Van Leeuwen, 2001, pp. 21–22). These presuppositions generally reflect cultural expectations of what "should" or "did" happen in language socialization long before the in-school learner ever met a science textbook (see Chapter 5 for more on language socialization).

A social semiotic theory of multimodalities pushes ethnographers to take an interest in "the social place, the history and formation of the sign-makers, and in the social environments in which they make their signs" (Kress & Street, 2006, p. viii). Ethnographers unpack and explicate both general and specific multimodalities as they look beyond the immediate situation to broad forces that create learning environments and their artifacts (see Scribner & Cole, 1981, for a classic study of "looking beyond" the immediate production of particular forms and functions of literacy). We have many affordances or possibilities of machine and human in meaning-making within the "borderless flows of data, information and image that characterise information economies" (Luke & Carrington, 2002, p. 247). Therefore, we must continuously update, refine, and expand methods of data collection and data analysis. We also have to reappraise given theories and develop new theories of explanation for events and practices, meanings and representations, on which actors call as they do their work of meaning-making in multiple situations of learning.

Summary

As Roger talks about how he learned to juggle and how he now sometimes tries to help others learn, Molly, his ethnographer, makes an inventory of all his modes of learning. She also observes Roger in practice, listens when he talks to others about his latest adventure in juggling, and watches him sit silently in a coffee shop, tossing small wads of paper from hand to hand. Molly notes not only the types of oral and written language Roger uses but also other modalities on which he draws. As anthropologist Judith Okely (1983) suggests in her ethnography of traveller gypsies in the United Kingdom: "Verbalisation is only one among other sources of meaning . . . gestures, positionings and silences in their contexts, all clues for a composite understanding" (p. 45).

In subsequent chapters, as we work toward "a composite understanding" of Roger as a juggler, we return to both Molly and Roger. At this point, however, we pull together just those means of information input and skill development that we heard Roger talk about in the opening of this chapter. In these few quotations, Roger tells Molly that he does the following:

1. He observes an intimate—a friend—and is motivated to try juggling, a "cool thing."
2. He reads about juggling.

3. He continues to observe others, try on his own, and self-assess and reflect on how he thinks he is doing. He acknowledges that much of his learning comes "just by trial and error."
4. He senses that he is feeling and embodying "the obvious" through his continued practice; he gains "muscle memory."
5. He creates and devises his own ways to practice and to learn effectively. He figures out the value of throwing the balls higher. He devises a way to use a wall to help him keep control of the balls. He acknowledges that he comes to feel "I could get on it [the ineluctable sense of control of the balls] well, standing with a wall next to me."
6. He comes to know "what it feels like" through emulating others in their juggling.

We have all watched jugglers, marveling at their dexterity and ability to make what they do look easy. We can see juggling as analogous to undertaking ethnography in the study of language and literacy. In the chapters ahead, we stay with the idea of juggling as we specify practices and principles of ethnography.

NOTES

1. Throughout this volume, the ethnographic work of Molly Mills in studying Roger (a pseudonym) is used with permission. We acknowledge with gratitude Molly's willingness to provide not only transcripts of her digital sound recordings of Roger but also insights into her own processes as a young social scientist exploring for the first time how to work and think as an ethnographer studying learning with particular attention to uses of oral language and other modalities. Molly carried out her study of Roger through observations, informal conversations, and interviews conducted between September and December 2006. She did her ethnographic work to fulfill a requirement for an Anthropology of Education course taught by Shirley at Brown University.

2. Our conventions related to use of quotation marks and italicized words denote a central dilemma within the social sciences. Many of the concepts and methods that these disciplines regard as belonging to *research* have widespread usage in popular journalism and the

creative arts (see Chapter 6 for more discussion on this point). In this volume, when we refer to words and phrases drawn from these broad popular and often everyday uses, we use quotation marks. When we use words or phrases that carry specific technical meanings within the social science disciplines, we italicize these so that they will stand out within the text as a whole. We generally italicize these terms only upon their first appearance within each chapter or when we want to emphasize the technical research-based meaning of the term.

3. Theories of structures of formal schooling, involvement of state systems, and conflicts between overt and hidden curricula come from scholars, such as Pierre Bourdieu, Suzanne deCastell, Henry Giroux, Herve Varenne, Raymond McDermott, Peter McLaren, and Hugh Mehan. "Critical literacy" studies share theoretical starting points with scholars who extend their work beyond the institutions of schooling to governmental bureaucracy, employment opportunities, and medical service delivery. A notable difference, however, lies in the fact that the work of critical literacy scholars centers on distinctions between "Discourse" (sharing much in definition with "Culture" but focusing on signs and symbols) and "discourse" (defined in its ordinary usage as a stretch of units of language). Major figures within critical literacy include James Gee, Colin Lankshear, and those within the New London Group, including Courtney Cazden, Allen Luke, Brian Street, and others. Intellectual histories of these groups may be found in Cope & Kalantzis, 2000; Gee, 1990/1996, 2000; Gee, Hull, & Lankshear, 1996; Hull & Schultz, 2002; Lankshear, 1997; Lankshear & Knobel, 2003; New London Group, 1996; Street, 1993a.

CHAPTER 2

The Ethnographer's Field Entry and Tools of Practice

The attachment, the identification, the uncertainty, the mystique, and perhaps above all, the ambivalence. (Jackson, 1990, p. 33)

As an ethnographer, Molly Mills studied Roger as he juggled and talked about his self-chosen identity. In the first weeks of her research, Molly's mind wandered. She found herself caught up in childhood memories. Weren't jugglers like clowns, tricksters, and fools? Didn't they run away from home to join the circus? Could she really be putting an academic lens on the frivolity of juggling? What started her on this quest? Was it her own curiosity about how, as a child, she had learned to play the violin while her friends pursued less challenging options?

Molly watched Roger as he practiced next to a wall and tried his hand with new combinations and numbers of balls. She listened as he refused to describe juggling as anything other than "disappointingly easy." None of this made sense even as Molly began to compare Roger's actions and talk of learning with what others did and said in their self-chosen learning of complex pursuits. She looked for what was common as well as different in their uses of words, pictures, and practices. She read everything she could find on learning complex mathematically based physical skills. She fretted that while Roger denied that actual mathematical calculations were part of what he did, his talk about juggling was full of technical vocabulary, explanations of physical properties, and what he called "intuitions" about how patterns work under conditions of change.

Molly collected masses of data: transcripts, fieldnotes, books on juggling, and notes from informal conversations with others. She had started out to study how learning happens as an individual decides to gain expertise in highly complex learning challenges. What she found led her to need to know what others had concluded on this topic and how they had accounted for learners' uses of patterns of symbolic structure, contradictory self-representations, and ambiguities about what could and should be known about their own skills.

Most of us as ethnographers identify with Molly. Ambivalence, uncertainty, and a curious attachment to figuring out what is happening keep ethnographers wanting to learn what others just accept or never really think about. Yet ethnographers know also that they are "invaders" of a certain sort, picking up and putting down facts and feelings of others, while simultaneously reflecting on their own memories and ideas. Even something seemingly so trivial as juggling had turned out for Molly to be locked in learner convictions and hidden within obvious practices.

The quote that opens this chapter comes from anthropologist Jean E. Jackson, who in the 1980s undertook a series of interviews on ways that ethnographers created, used, and rethought the genre of fieldnotes. Reflections on this genre, so central to the work of ethnographers, circled through ethnographers' joyous and yet ambiguous travails from entering a chosen field site to writing up their fieldnotes. In this chapter, we address at the outset how we think most ethnographers insert themselves into their chosen work. We then consider the ways they select their field site. We look at how ethnographers determine their tools of practice and keep in mind core research values, such as those surrounding *reliability*, *replicability*, and *validity*.

We suggest that the ways in which these tools and values have developed within ethnography are critically distinct from those of *qualitative research* more generally. This latter term embraces one or more of the face-to-face methods of inquiry (such as interviewing) and stresses the epistemological foundations of research based on these methods. Often absent, however, is grounding of chosen methods in theoretical perspectives or conceptual frameworks from a particular social science discipline.

In contrast, ethnography as genre and goal relies on some linkage with or acknowledgment of its history within anthropology and its subfields, such as linguistics. Ethnography, as we see in subsequent chapters, is a theory-building enterprise constructed through detailed systematic observing, recording, and analyzing of human behavior in specifiable spaces and interactions. In this volume, we do not equate ethnography with qualitative research, as some methodologists do (cf. Hammersley & Atkinson, 1995, p. 2). As you read ethnographers' accounts, from the field entry issues detailed in this chapter, to the ethnographic practices of fieldwork described in Chapters 3 and 4, keep in mind a search for distinctions. Doing so will help you work out for yourself exactly how you see the relationship between qualitative research more generally and ethnography in particular.

ENTERING THE FIELD:
SHIRLEY GOES TO TRACKTON AND ROADVILLE

To undertake ethnography is to enter willingly into a messy set of tasks that will continue over a considerable period of time among strangers that the ethnographer may inevitably "betray." Field research has been described as "an act of betrayal, no matter how well intentioned or well integrated the researcher." Consequently, the ultimate "business" of the ethnographer "makes public the private and leaves the locals to take the consequences" (Miles & Huberman, 1984, p. 233).

What opens ethnographers to the idea of undertaking their particular study? If pushed hard enough, most ethnographers admit that a sense of curiosity and adventure, a desire to know, a sense of "real" unknowns take them to the field. Moreover, within every such researcher rests a core concern about the quality and integrity of human life. (See, for example, anthropologist Margaret Mead's introductions to Mead, 1930, 1956; see especially pp. 31–35, 1956, on knowing "what literacy is."). We thus begin this chapter not with the usual advice that ethnographers start with a "good" research question but rather the reminder that is a refrain throughout this volume: As you collect data, know the company you keep as ethnographer and get to know yourself as constant learner—ever curious and open to what's happening. Remember always that we study something because we already know something.

The opener that led to *Ways with Words: Language, Life and Work in Communities and Classrooms* (Heath, 1983/1996b), a book often seen as centered on language, came from knowing that the political dimensions of the late 1960s were wiping away social and historical realities. When the civil rights movement and desegregation came to the southeastern United States in the late 1960s, most White teachers had had lifelong and almost daily interactions with Blacks of their region. Yet the communicative underpinnings of these relationships suddenly seemed to disappear when White teachers claimed they could not understand the talk of Black children in their classrooms.

Further "new" proclamations came in local newspapers and from Black and White teachers alike: Black children could not speak "proper" or "standard" English; they did not listen well; and they came to school without skills in counting, identifying, and classifying. Yet in all rural and small-town areas of the Southeast, every radio station carried programs in which local and national Black speakers shifted back and forth across varieties of English. The civil rights movement had generated more widespread attention to the oratorical powers of Black speakers than at any other time in American history.

Moreover, every merchant in small towns knew well the counting, identifying, and classifying skills of children, Black and White, who were sent to stores by their caregiving grand-parents with whom the children stayed while parents worked. In the springtime, these children knew how to distinguish one type of plant seedling from another, one kind of hoe from another, and what the count should be on certain pharmaceutical prescriptions they were sent to the drugstore to collect. In many parts of the Southeast, every White knew members of the Black middle class whose linguistic repertories exceeded their own. Periods in military service, residence in northern cities, or extensive travel in connection with their professions had expanded the number of dialects, languages, and styles of talking of the numerous Blacks who sought opportunities outside the Southeast after World War II.

Shirley's study of language socialization in southeastern communities, both Black and White, initially seemed to be about language. *Ways with Words*, however, ultimately proved to be about integrity and quality of life and the need to understand how long-standing personal human relationships slip away under political and social pressures. This illustration of what can open a desire for fieldwork in a particular place and time underscores the fact that within ethnography, the researcher is the instrument.

Though much is said about *participant observation* as the key means of collecting data as an ethnographer, the truth is that only rarely can we shed features of ourselves to be a "real" participant. Molly was not a juggler; struggling to learn to be one could help her talk with Roger, but she could never take on features that emerged as central in Roger's identity of himself as juggler. Ethnography forces us to think consciously about ways to enter into the life of the individual, group, or institutional life of the "other." (For more on how the history of anthropology in the early 20th century introduced the idea of ethnographer-as-participant-observer, see Chapter 6.)

What ethnographers really want to know is "What is happening here in the field site(s) I have chosen?" This question asks not just for a description of events and actions that people create, react to, assess, and learn within but also for history and explanations informed by and leading to theories. What does the ethnographer find when tracing the lines of connection for what is heard, said, and done by an individual such as Roger the juggler? What about the study of groups that interact in their own communities in historically established ways while meanwhile denying knowledge drawn from habits they have followed all their lives? How do people adapt when their daily lives shift radically as a result of decisions brought about by social forces and institutions over which they have little or no control?

THE CONSTANT COMPARATIVE

Since ethnographers always work somewhere within a series of interlocking circles, they have to keep looking in multiple ways and directions. They look at individuals as they learn, to be sure, but they also have to see how these learners locate themselves within groups of identity-makers and in relation to influential formal institutions.

Ethnographic research has come to mean "making the familiar strange," a term probably first used by the 18th-century German poet-philosopher Friedrich von Hardenberg and circulated later by William Wordsworth, Samuel Taylor Coleridge, and T. S. Eliot. Most anthropologists know the idea with respect to what the ethnographer is supposed to do (Agar, 1980/1996). But, in any situation, before tackling the documentation of the "strange," the ethnographer has to know as much as possible about the "familiar." This means using accurate observation to find out what is already known—and to whom, for what, and under what kinds of circumstances.

This kind of finding-out in the work of ethnographers depends on a *constant comparative perspective* that cuts to the past and to the future of the topic or area under study. In the present chapter, we develop what we mean by the constant comparative through considering the ethnographer's place and tools of practice. This chapter parallels the next in that readers should move back and forth as they focus simultaneously on literature reviews and methods of data collection. Once an ethnographer chooses a topic or area, the best preparation for fieldwork is to learn everything possible about what others have written and argued that may be relevant. Here the tricky word is "relevant."

Molly needed to know much more about the mathematics of juggling than she bargained for when the idea of studying a juggler came to her. She also did not expect to have to read books on complex problem solving, practical intelligence, or embodied learning. She read general studies of "unschooled" types of expertise, such as that characterizing waitresses, plumbers, dancers, and actors. She read about how to do ethnography, what anthropology of education was and had been, and she talked to several anthropologists who studied learning. As she began her collection of data through observing and listening, she came to see books from more "distant" fields, such as theater and gesture, as "relevant." This back-and-forth observing, noting, reading, thinking, observing, and noting constitute data collection toward fieldwork as an ethnographer. Consider that this may well be a set of practices distinguishing ethnography from other forms of "qualitative" research, such as classroom observation or interviews that may be less recursive, with less back-and-forth among historical, comparative, and current fieldwork sources.

What are the theories, field sites, and findings of past and contemporary work related to the ethnographer's chosen topic? Ethnographers often note the sentiment that "non-field" sources suggest lines of questioning and topics to pursue in fieldwork (cf. Lederman, 1990, p. 76). Because much of any ethnographic pursuit is driven by curiosity about aspects of human behavior, building an intellectual framework that defines and legitimizes the topic or area of attraction for the individual researcher is essential. Otherwise, the original impetus may drift away or come to seem silly and trivial even to the ethnographer. This is why questions that center on behaviors that can be documented, quantified, compared, and analyzed through various theories need to scaffold original hunches or impulses (see Figure 2.1).

Figure 2.1. The Recursive Process in Doing Ethnography:
Theory and Practice

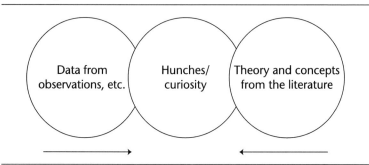

This recursive process also reminds us that we can no longer play on the perhaps still publicly perceived tropes of "innocent ethnographer" who enters the field with a mind clear of
all presuppositions ready to take part as "full" member. Rather
we acknowledge our original hunches and test these against
the findings of other researchers. We also enter our field site(s)
open to learning. As we do so, we keep in mind the many limitations we bring as instrument. Our physical features (such as
age, gender, size, and phenotype), as well as our own cultural
identities and life experiences, prevent our fully participating
as the "other." Reflexivity, rather than innocence, characterizes contemporary ethnography. (For more on this point, see
Chapter 6.)

An ethnographer intending to study patterns of interaction surrounding structures and uses of language and literacy
has, then, first to find out about the data that other researchers have used to support their theories. Once in the field, the
ethnographer keeps this information in mind while observing,
listening, and recording. Molly wanted to know more about
learners who take on tasks leading to an area of self-selected
expertise. She read all that she could find about self-motivated
learning of cognitively complex tasks. She noted how other
researchers had gone about studying such situations.

As she did so, she refined the central data collection tasks of her initial fieldwork; she wanted data that would answer basic questions. What are the identifiable features that characterize how Roger moves through any given day? How, when, and where does juggling enter into each day's activities, times, and spaces? What are the distinctive, definable, and quantifiable features of situations in which Roger self-identifies as juggler? The ability to ask such questions comes from studying the following:

1. Case studies of other jugglers
2. Comparative cases of individuals who decide on their own to become experts in other highly technical manual and mental accomplishments
3. Technical accounts and mathematical representations of juggling
4. Theories of learning that relate to everyday learning of complex skill sets

Note that Molly did not ask *why* Roger was learning juggling. Most ethnographers stick with questions of who, when, what, where, and how. The fundamental challenge to ethnographers is to lay out *what is happening. Why* questions are teleological in nature and resist proof by empirical means. The goals of the social sciences, including anthropology, do not conform to the interests of foregone conclusions based in faith and value judgments about what is "true," "wonderful," or "good," or what is "false," "ugly," or "evil."

Collecting data and mindfully contrasting aspects of time, space, material objects, actors, and interactional routines call for close observation and consistent recording. Conceptual frames for analyzing such data derive from knowledge that the ethnographer has gained from other case studies, readings of theories of learning, and prior areas of specialized training for the ethnographer (e.g., extent of knowledge of linguistics).

Most ethnographers focus initially on similarities that occur across different times and under varying sets of circumstances within the chosen research situation. By gaining a sense of what is predictable and familiar to those within the local field site, ethnographers begin to see patterns of local behaviors and beliefs that generally lie outside the awareness of the interactants. Yet deep respect for local knowledge by those living or working in the field site is crucial. These individuals have a lifetime of responding with precision and predictability to the minutiae of their everyday lives. This is true even though they may not see the need for or be able to identify and explain these patterns through specifics of *how, what,* and so on. This point holds even when a highly specialized field of knowledge and set of skills have passed from one generation to the next (c.f. Greenfield, 2004).

In describing similarities, ethnographers follow a fundamental rule in data collection: "Describe only what does happen, not what does not happen." Researchers unaccustomed to working in a cross-cultural or constant comparative frame often fall into the ethnocentric trap of claiming: "They do x and we do y, or we do x and they do not."

To illustrate the error of ethnocentrism, Buddhists use several versions of the story of the turtle and fish. One story goes like this:

> One day the turtle decides to go for a walk on dry land. He is away from the lake for a few weeks. When he returns, he meets some fish who ask him: "Mister Turtle, hello! We have not seen you for a few weeks. Where have you been?" The turtle says, "I was up on the dry land." The fish are puzzled: "Up on dry land? What is this dry land? Is it wet?" The turtle answers "No, it is not." "Is it cool and refreshing?" the fish ask. "No it is not." "Does it have waves and ripples?" "No, it does not have waves and ripples." "Can you swim in it?" "No, you cannot." So the fish say: "It is not wet, it is not cool, there are no waves, you can't swim in it. So this dry land of yours must be completely non-existent, just an imaginary thing, nothing real at all." The turtle says: "Well, that may be so," and he leaves the fish and goes for another walk on dry land.

(www.beyondthenet/dhamma/nibbanaTurtle.htm. Accessed April 2007).

We as ethnographers might think of this story in a briefer form. When the turtle returns from dry land to water, and the fish question him, the turtle answers only by saying that the land has no waves, no seaweed, and so on. The fish admonish: "Don't tell us what it's *not*, tell us what it *is!*" The longer version of the story is more hopeful than our brief account, for the turtle takes with him on his return "walk on dry land" refined questions and the intention to see what is there this time.

The tendency to note what is not occurring comes from a fundamental orientation toward value judgment; perhaps humans (and turtles) have a natural response to see other situations and actions only in terms of their own. Humans (and fish) can discount as imaginary or simply nonexistent evidence they neither recognize nor wish to entertain within their worldview.

The tendency to make value judgments and to discount information that does not fit a current frame of reference reflects the common idea that *comparing* is the same activity or process as *contrasting*. The latter, more than the former, accounts for similarities and differences in terms of their labels, characteristics, uses, and contexts. When asked to *compare* one restaurant's pizza with another's, respondents generally offer judgments about merits: "Well, I think A's pizza is better; it fills me up more, and I always leave feeling satisfied." The question "How would you *contrast* the pizza served in restaurant A with that of restaurant B?" brings answers that include details about crust, contents, amount of topping, size of servings, and so on.

Every ethnographer must always be on guard against letting one's own beliefs about what *should be* overcome the accuracy of detailing what *is*. Molly was curious about juggling, and she brought to her study some long-standing judgments about what juggling was. She had to learn that ethnography is not a playground for either being blind to what is happening, or for "proving" one's own values or beliefs. Ethnography, as noted earlier, is a theory-building and theory-dependent enterprise. Ethnographers construct, test, and amplify theoretical perspectives through systematic observing, recording, and analyzing of human behavior in specifiable spaces and interactions. It is the ethnographer's job to detail those spaces and interactions for the co-occurrence of language, literacy, and multimodalities for any situation or context selected as field site(s).

CO-OCCURRENCES FOR PATTERN DETECTION: SHIRLEY FIGURES OUT HOW SKATEBOARDERS TELL TIME

The best way to get around the tendency either to contrast or to compare in simplistic ways is to keep in mind that the *constant comparative* calls for vigilance to *co-occurrence*. What happens as something else happens? How do such events take place similarly again and again? When does a particular pattern of events or process for one or another phenomenon seem out of sync with established habits? When does behavior show some kind of variation from what others say they do or will "always" happen? Anthropologists learn, in practice, to rely on the fact that ideals and conventions often become evident only when the anthropologist unwittingly breaks these local "rules" and therefore needs rebuke, instruction, and guidance from those who are "in the know" (cf. Okely, 1983, pp. 44–45).

As the fieldworker searches for *co-occurrences*, patterns emerge that lie outside either the consciousness or the concern of locals, who often view as self-evident and foolish the work that ethnographers undertake to unravel patterns of behavior and their contexts.

For example, Shirley found in her study of how young people establish and manage their own learning environments outside of family and school that skateboarders in one urban area always showed up late at night at a specific location within minutes of one another. Yet none wore watches or showed any obvious way of keeping close track of time, and members of the group came via different modes of transport. This precision of timing seemed curious to Shirley, since the young people reported of themselves (and others confirmed the same idea) that they did not care about time and, in fact, took pride in not showing up "on time" for anything. Months passed before Shirley could figure out just how they were so precise in their synchronized arrivals. She records this ethnographic "aha!" in her personal reflections that run parallel to her fieldnotes (a technique Brian and Shirley recommend and illustrate in Chapter 4).

I have finally unraveled the details of predictability that govern their consistent "on time" behavior each night at the skate park. After many rereadings of fieldnotes, I realized that the boys talk frequently about a particular television series that was either previewed or shown each week at the same time on a station widely available in the area. I then hypothesized that perhaps the skateboarders' enthusiasm for the show led them in their various neighborhoods to collect in front of television stores to watch the preview spot or the show together. The next few nights, I checked this out, and indeed this was the case. Therefore, wherever they were in the city, as the time for the television show approached, they checked out television stores to gauge the actual distance from their skateboarding area. Once the television show was over, they headed for their favorite skateboard location. They all knew how long it would take them to get to the skateboard area from the particular television stores along their routes through the city. Thus they "planned" accordingly. By this time of night, their chosen location of practice would be relatively free of interference by the police who kept them away during daylight hours when their fast moves and seemingly erratic patterns threatened tourists. But their city had a curfew requiring all young people under 18 to be off the streets on week nights by 1 A.M. Therefore their "being on time" (my phrase—not theirs) ensured a certain amount of practice time before they had to disperse.

Putting together such a disparate set of details is necessary in any field site to determine patterns and the co-occurring features of their context. In Shirley's case, she uncovered not only the means by which the young men's behaviors reflected predictable timing but also a coalescence of common interests that "bound" the group together beyond the purview of their skateboarding location. Moreover, the groups had to have some conscious awareness of how long it would take to get from their different television viewing points scattered around the city to the designated skateboarding area.

Shirley's analysis of detail centered on being able to note patterns of *co-occurrence.* Transcriptions of conversations of the young men when they broke their skateboarding practice for a smoke finally revealed the critical detail that they had a favorite television show in common. Shirley needed this detail of patterned interaction to determine the unspoken coordination behind the boys' precision in their arrival time.

Yet no member of the group ever articulated this set of strategies, nor, in the end, did they even see Shirley's "finding" as being of any significance at all. Shirley's reflections near the end of the study record the following:

> This evening, knowing I might not see the boys again for several months, I debriefed them on what I had learned by hanging out at their skateboard spot for so many months. One thing I told them was how I had solved my early puzzlement over their coordinated punctuality. Their faces registered no trace of surprise or positive acknowledgment of what I regarded as quite a piece of detective work. Instead, they turned immediately to talking about this particular television show and asking me what I thought of it. They ended this portion of the debriefing by saying, almost in chorus: "Yeah, hey, we don't miss that show!"

What the boys did to get themselves to the park on time was so routine and logical to them that they found nothing special in the fact that someone else had unlocked this set of behaviors. Yet for Shirley, her detective work uncovered strategies of coordination for the young men around both entertainment and their insistence on the need for practice in skateboarding. Both of these activities were important enough to ensure coming together as a big group in a certain place at a particular time—something outsiders believed "they could never do."

In terms of methods of work, all Shirley did as an ethnographer was to take note of one particular feature of the young men's interaction (arrival time) and then set about to determine what else was going on simultaneously in the in-transit blocks of time of the different groups. She asked of her fieldnotes and her observations: What else is going on at the same time? How frequently does it occur and under what circumstances? To have asked the boys why they always came on time would have produced points already obvious, such as "we want to," "it matters," or "got to get there when the cops aren't around." The big question was *how?* Searching out *co-occurrences* lies at the heart of the *constant comparative* ethos and approach of ethnographers. This search will mean dealing with a number of levels and domains of knowledge over which locals have out-of-awareness expertise.

Useful to keep in mind is the well-known reflection of anthropologist Clifford Geertz (1973) on the power of "thick description" to get at the patterns behind how a specific action takes place in terms of its context. But describing deeply will not do everything for the ethnographer. In reflecting on his career, Geertz (2005) mused that his early life "predisposed me to becoming, in both life and work, the seeker after a pattern, however fragmentary, amid a swirl of accident. . . . I assumed, and I still assume, that what you are supposed to do is keep going with whatever you can find lying about to keep going with: to get from yesterday to today without foreclosing tomorrow" (p. 123). The capacity and will to keep going in the search derive from the researcher as instrument with a history and a drive toward resolving the puzzle of where fragments can lead.

Resisting Preconceptions

Only with the *constant comparative* and *co-occurrence* can the ethnographer get beyond everyday preconceptions about a particular group or situation. Skateboarders in their local community were widely regarded as "slough-offs," "school failures," and "kids who aren't coming to any good in life." When questioned, community members always noted that "these kids" failed in school and would never be able to hold down jobs. Punctuality, dress, respect behaviors, and "caring about something that matters" were features often denied as characterizing the skateboarders. Therefore, when precision in punctuality showed up consistently in Shirley's data, this feature jumped out in terms of the need for explication through constant comparative analysis. Shirley's avoidance of this negative preconception is what allowed her to probe into the management of these evening skateboard gatherings—just as Brian's response to negative preconceptions about the "illiteracy" of Iranian villagers prompted him to follow through to learn what was "really going on" (see Chapter 3).

The theoretical implications of Shirley's "finding" echo the studies of effective out-of-school or after-school learning environments concluding that "making time matter" defines the dedication of the young. If young people know that being late makes a difference that is "real" to them, they find ways to be punctual. For play rehearsals, sports practices, and community service meetings with officials who listen, most young people show up on time. When punctuality rules seem arbitrary or link to nothing that has meaning for them, young people often have erratic patterns of arrival. For example, when the window of time for use of a highly prized sound system is limited, and the youth band has access only during this brief span, members show up on time. Rules merit respect and response when they tie to opportunities for meaningful practice and performance. The skateboarders valued their physical and temporal location and thus each embraced the responsibility to arrive on time. In so doing, they displayed dedication to a group meaningful to them despite the considerable risk of the activity.

It is often the case that ethnographers "uncover" rule-governed behaviors, norms of interaction, and complex skills for groups or activities previously unacknowledged, unsanctioned, or thought of in entirely different ways. Such was the case for child vendors on the streets of Brazilian favelas who engaged daily in intricate mathematical calculations (Nunes, Schliemann, & Caraher, 1993; Saxe, 1988). Work on "street mathematics" stimulated educators to look anew at their earlier ideas about "remedial" instruction in mathematics needed for children from underresourced communities.

Eglash and his colleagues (2006), for instance, build upon such "ethnomathematics" to examine the performance and engagement of underrepresented minority students in school mathematics. The team works with students using Culturally Situated Design Tools (CSDT) to link their everyday knowledge with that of the school curriculum. Web-based applets, developed by students and tutors in collaboration, call upon mathematical knowledge embedded in cultural designs such as cornrow hairstyles, Native American beadwork, Latino percussion rhythms, and so on. CSDT allows students to use these underlying mathematical principles to simulate specific enquiries in calculation and design. This work indicates ways in which educators call upon basic ethnographic work to build learning on students' prior cultural knowledge (see also Street, Baker, & Tomlin, 2005).

This approach raises issues of *emic* and *etic* knowledge that run through this book: individual and group knowledge may be implicit or explicit in the design and execution of highly complex practices, such as creating beadwork and hairstyles or juggling and skateboarding. An *etic* or *constant-comparative* perspective enables us to understand underlying actions and their co-occurring patterns and contextual features. The *emic* or locally held perspective of an individual, group, or institution, such as a school, can bring into its knowledge system that which has been established from an *etic* or comparative analysis. The complex algorithms in creating hairstyles or bead patterns, selling in street stalls, and juggling come to the surface with *etic* work and make such knowledge available for the use of others. In Chapter 6, we explore ethical dilemmas that come from such "sharing," as well as the growing need for subjects and researchers to collaborate. Together, they must determine the revelation of "insider" or *emic* knowledge to "outsiders." We would suggest that any ethnographic statement will be, to quote Michael Agar (1980/1996), a blend of "assumptions about perceptions or intent on the part of group members" as well as the ethnographer's background knowledge of related literatures and past research. We should always remember that the original sense of *emic* and *etic* "captures this blending and calls our attention to it" (pp. 239–240).

RELIABILITY, REPLICABILITY, AND VALIDITIES

Ethnographers undertaking "the art of fieldwork" struggle with questions *of validity, reliability, and replicability.* The kind of *reliability* called for in other social sciences—that which requires the same response to the same stimuli on repeated occasions—is not expected in ethnographers' study of daily life. *Replicability* seems similarly out of reach for ethnographers, since every field immersion is by definition unique. The in-the-moment ongoing cycle of events of any group is never identical upon repetition, nor is the individual ethnographer as a research instrument replicable in other individuals.

Since the 1980s, ethnographers have dealt with the problems of *reliability* and *replicability* in increasingly sophisticated ways through exemplary guides, models, and "methodological explorations" in ethnographic fieldwork. Some of these sound a cautionary note while others celebrate the depth and theoretical generativity of ethnographic work (Agar, 1980/1996; Hammersley, 1992; Hammersley & Atkinson, 1995; Wolcott, 2001). In addition, several key articles "translate" the difficulties that ethnographers in specific fields, such as education, face in the context of comparison with those who do experimental research or survey-based work (e.g., Dobbert & Kurth-Schai, 1992; Eisenhart & Howe, 1992; Green & Bloome, 1997).

Underlying this chapter has been the accepted view that all ethnographic research is inherently interpretive, subjective, and partial. Thus what matters is that researchers lay out *decision rules* that guide how they do their work. The ethnographer must recognize that comparison between one study and another can only be based on descriptions of who, what, where, when, and how. Time moves on, people change, and circumstances differ, yet ethnographers have an obligation to make clear their *decision rules* as though they could imagine that someone else might step back into the same location or group.

In essence, a number of keen criteria hold for ethnographers; central among these are those of *comparison* and *contrast*. How well do the data stand up to what we know from other places? If the data show similarities and differences with other studies, then does the ethnographer offer reasonable explanations for this? Two kinds of *validity* lie at the center of decision rules—*empirical* and *theoretical validity*. The first asks us to ensure that we can answer the questions of whether or not the data "add up" and whether they back up the claims made. The second—*theoretical validity*—calls on us to feel confident that the account resulting from our work can stand up to critiques of the theories we have deployed or of those we posit (cf. Eisenhart & Howe, 1992).

To be sure, readers often speak of the *validity* of the work of ethnographers in terms of whether the situations and scenes depicted come alive or not. In methodological terms, the basis of this judgment relies on the extent to which ethnographers convey *co-occurrence* through rich details of time, space, artifacts, and interactants. Central to such co-occurrence is communication—whether gestural, musical, dramatic, or verbal.

Visual and performative dimensions of communication have to ring true in terms of interlocutors as well as audience and eavesdroppers.

In earlier decades, it was common for ethnographers to think of their field site as a fixed location. For many reasons, today's ethnographers, especially those who study learning, may follow individuals or groups that are on the move. Ethnographers can follow one phenomenon, such as ballet (Wulff, 1998) or one year's graduating class from a particular secondary school (Ortner, 2005). Some study women in relation to specific media-promoted issues or problems (Eisenhart & Finkel, 1998; Holland & Eisenhart, 1990). Some study multiple locations (Hannerz, 2003; Marcus, 1995, 1998). Some do comparative work on phenomena generally seen as the domain of other disciplines, such as governance (Shore & Wright,1997), organizational life (Wright,1994), or violence (Nordstrom & Robben, 1995). Nevertheless, more often than not, individuals reflecting unique and creative combinations of tactics and strategies in their learning remain a key focus of attention for ethnographers. How these individuals interact not only with artifacts and physical environments but also with other individuals and social norms lies at the heart of questions that motivate ethnographers.

Regardless of the individual, group, or moving and multiple field sites, ethnographers will benefit as they prepare proposals for their work from thinking through some early-stage *decision rules*. The questions below indicate the nature of these decisions and should stand out in the mind of any ethnographer proposing fieldwork.

- Who or what is the phenomenon of central focus? What are salient features?
- Who am I with respect to these individuals, the group, or the sites?
- What will the times and spaces of data collecting be?
- What makes me curious about what is happening here? How would I answer someone who asks about the one or two

central issues or experiences in my own life that have led to my being here?

- What will I consistently be able to tell others about who I am and what I will be doing here?
- How will I protect the identity and interests of those whose lives I propose to examine?

To be sure, once the proposal has been completed, there will be other decision rules to make that will guide the data collection, as well as analysis and presentation of research results. Later chapters indicate some of these decision rules that apply from literature reviews through data collection and on to production of written, oral, or visual genres reporting the research.

SUMMARY

This chapter has tried to make sense of Roger's stated convictions about his own learning and Molly's challenges in tackling her initial curiosity about how people go about learning self-chosen highly complex tasks. Ethnographic work is one of these highly complex tasks.

Just as Roger goes back and forth between actual practice, reading books and watching others, building models in his head, and thinking of what he might do to improve, so ethnographers engage in similar zigzag work from start to finish. They must read all they can about their area of curiosity, think ahead about what is realistic and practical to achieve, and learn how to explain their endeavor in clear, concise ways. Initial selection of relevant materials before even entering the chosen field site helps to focus the research. The questions at the core of an ethnographer's essential curiosity will inspire an opening up to the learning that comes from the places and tools of the work ahead.

CHAPTER 3

Setting Decision Rules
for Fieldwork

> Ethnographic fieldwork involves a series of choices. These choices and the theoretical reasons for them need to be presented explicitly to establish ethnographic validity. (Sanjek, 1990, p. 395)

In the last chapter, we left Molly figuring out where her work as an ethnographer was beginning and how it could move forward. Having started with an interest in how motivation and incentive from a childhood friend launched Roger into juggling, Molly now wondered what really started her off in ethnography.

She thought about the parallel she found in her own life with what Roger was doing. She had studied violin, at the urging of her parents, for years, but she had decided, after starting college, to give up the violin. But, while watching Roger in his juggling, she decided to start playing again. Now in her study and her own music, she kept hearing some of Roger's first words of introduction to his juggling:

> "It looks better when you do the alternation."
> "I actually learned how to do that by messing up."
> "When you're walking, my theory is that you're kind of auto-correcting anyway, because you're not at one balance point when you're walking . . . so on the slack-line, your body is more conscious of trying to balance."

Molly wondered if in her years of classical instruction, she had gone on "autocorrect." Now she informally "practiced" with other musicians who enjoyed improvising; she worked with those who called themselves "fiddlers" and those who took pleasure in not being able to "read" music. She relished opportunities to play in groups featuring instruments and styles she had never before heard. Perhaps these unusual settings were her equivalent of Roger's taking his juggling from sidewalk to slack-line or unicycle. In both ethnography and in her music, she could not operate on automatic now, for every improvised session invigorated her with new consciousness of music, relationship to her instrument, and sense of interdependence. She had to make conscious to herself and others some fundamental rules of operation for the learning ahead.

———

A deep secret of most ethnographers is the fact that their most productive questions come from a true curiosity. This curiosity moves them into different literatures as they think about collecting data. Choice of individual, situation, and physical location of fieldwork ties closely and even logically with this desire for increasing knowledge through reading as well as looking and listening. Sometimes one individual or situation may be just as good as another for satisfying the ethnographer's urge to learn about a particular phenomenon. Often more than one location provides answers, leading ethnographers to undertake multisite research simultaneously (cf. Hannerz, 2003; Marcus, 1998).

LITERATURE REVIEWS: THE COMPANY WE KEEP

Simultaneous with facing the concerns noted in Chapter 2, ethnographers writing research proposals and preparing for fieldwork are reviewing literatures that bear some explicable relevance to the work being planned. All such reviews are iterative: initiating reviews before field entry, starting and stopping throughout data collection, letting go of entire bodies of work, acquiring and picking up others throughout the fieldwork and latter phases. One of the toughest points of cutoff in ethnographic work comes when we know we must stop reading what others have written and focus instead on the current writing challenge of the ethnographer. Molly's study of Roger was limited to one academic term. Yet we have some idea of the range of literatures that became relevant to her understanding of Roger as an instance of voluntary complex learning. Had she been studying, for example, festival jugglers in European cities as a collective group, the range of literatures relevant to her work would have been more extensive, as would have been her time in multiple field sites.

Often one hears about the *literature review* as though there were only one body of literature to review or that one could produce a single such review. We speak instead of *literature reviews* to emphasize both the iterative nature of such readings and the need to read across topics and even disciplines as central research questions get refined during the course of fieldwork. Though this zigzag nature of going back and forth from fieldwork to literature and back again may distinguish the ethnographers' work from that of most other social scientists, other aspects of ethnography also stand out as different. Ethnographers do not begin their research with a clearly defined research question or delimiting hypothesis. Taking their cue from anthropologists, ethnographers have field sites and areas of core interest in front of them as they begin their research, but they do not enter their work with a single fixed question. We must remember that the "charting of the ethnographic terrain is filtered through theory so that more selective and systematic participant observation will follow." Throughout fieldwork, the "net of people, place, and activities studied opportunistically may continue to widen in fieldnotes, but theory-guided research activities will narrow at the same time" (Sanjek, 1990, p. 396). Refinement of interest, methods, and situation come through thinking ahead, deliberating decision rules, then thinking back and recalibrating earlier such rules as the research moves forward and as one understands the relevant literatures more deeply through field experiences.

Consider, for example, someone setting out to write an ethnography of one or more situations or organizations in which several means of learning take place simultaneously. Instructor-led teaching happens and learners and instructor experiment together; engage in play (including joking, teasing, and occasional minidramas); talk about current news events and favorite foods; and do some interactive reading, writing, and talking in small groups along the way. Some school classrooms contain just such a jumble of activities, as do laboratories of software development firms and summer science camps. For an ethnographer studying any of these sites, it would be logical to select bodies of literature that include some or all of the following plus other materials relevant to the particular type of individuals, groups, or physical location of the site(s) selected:

1. Studies of "informal" learning and theoretical pieces distinguishing among terms such as "formal," "nonformal," or "informal," as well as "experiential," "practice-based," and so on
2. Literature on the role of joking and play within workplaces or sites of organizational learning
3. Works on critique within projects or ongoing learning within situations not governed entirely by assigned instructors or curricula
4. Reviews of "creativity" or "innovation" in learning situations or organizations, and the importance of give-and-take in the flow of activities to effective outcomes of "creative learning."

The purpose of any initial selection of relevant works is to determine what has already been done on one's phenomenon of central focus. Picking out subtopics, such as those above, with which to begin literature reviews comes from taking a dozen or so slices of behavior in a site and asking of each one: "What are the adjectives or nouns that pop into my head when I look at this incident?" In this way, terms such as "informal," "teasing," and "play" come to the surface for the setting noted above. Working through the literatures of these subtopics enables the ethnographer to figure out where holes and disagreements exist and to think about how the proposed work will supplement, resolve, and complement theories and information currently available.

Research, particularly when carried out for a graduate thesis, generally asks that scholars make an "original" contribution to the field. The term "original" can be very scary. However, such a contribution amounts to doing any one (and sometimes a combination) of several things that can range from creating an entirely new theory to clarifying and refining or even negating one or more existing theories.

The most important role of literature reviews is then to ensure that current work builds from existing knowledge. Every researcher stands on the shoulders of those who have gone before. In earlier decades, ethnographers looked to geographers, cartographers, and travelers' accounts before they headed off to villages or islands distant from their home countries (see Chapter 6). Shirley found the first chapter of *Ways with Words* (Heath, 1983/1996b) by far the most difficult to write, because she had to dig deep into records of textile mills in the Piedmont South, learning their labor practices and types of machinery (often available primarily through photographs and diagrams of mill interiors). Yet she knew she had to establish for herself and her readers the memories and daily realities of work in southern textile mills.

Ethnographers always face the challenge of where to look and what to read in order to situate their own current fieldwork. Reaching across disciplines is essential. "Interdisciplinarity" rings as a familiar term in the ear of every university student, but the questions remain of which disciplines, which authors, and where to start. Answers often come in ad hoc directions and generally depend on who and what university instructors or advisers know. Thus bibliographies often read like close-kin charts; if one name is included, clever readers will soon figure out the school, thrust, or positionality of the entire work. Ethnographers who study learning and the roles of language, literacy, and multimodalities in learning have to reach beyond the kin circles of their own instructors or advisers for their literature reviews. Often the most efficient way to reach more broadly is simply to track the meanings across fields of terms that seem to keep popping up. For example, in 2007, terms related to *embodied knowledge, embodiment, embodied interaction,* and *body and mind* kept appearing in the public media, education journals, and neuroscience reviews. An ethnographer setting out to study learning in 2007 could benefit from pursuing these ideas in several research literatures. What happens as learners take on or embody several roles in their daily lives or in the course of learning something new? For those working in multimodal literacies, a key aspect of this question relates to the inclusion of several modes of learning and displaying knowledge and skills. To what extent will observing and representing different forms such as those of the arts and sciences (e.g., sketches, photographs, computer simulations) figure in the course of achieving expertise in various roles?

Summation of one's reviews of literatures—taking place as the research is being proposed and also intermittently from start to finish of fieldwork—will include the following components:

1. Conceptual framework for the research in terms of relevant bodies of theory and reviews of prior field studies
2. Integrated coherent review of the major bodies of work selected
3. Buildup or lead-in to the current study through delineations of how this proposed research differs from that of others and leads toward original contributions to theory.

Though it may seem simplistic to think in this way, it is often helpful to know that the lead-in for any proposed research generally moves along one or more of the following lines:

1. What has gone before has been wrong, inadequate, never previously applied in certain sites, or examined through certain methods of data collection and analysis.
2. What has gone before—generally in theory development—is now reemerging in new ways and bears examination in particular sites through specific methods.
3. What has gone before has pointed in particular directions that have not previously been considered and now must be taken up because of contemporary pertinent issues, concerns, or policies.
4. What has gone before did not have the benefit of recent work in other disciplines, and therefore application of certain methods or theories from these disciplines to the problem or issue will amplify and strengthen past work.

Writing an engaging and effective review of the bodies of literature relevant for one's research, whether at the proposal stage or in the final write-up, calls for some commonsense strategies:

1. Build curiosity and attention to the central framework of the research by making the reader believe that a new and worthwhile journey lies ahead.
2. Demonstrate a clear, concise grasp of the conceptual bases of the literatures reviewed; do this by citing only what you have read thoroughly and carefully; never cite references that you have only found in someone else's bibliography.
3. Weave the lines of findings or interpretations of the literatures together into a scenario or story that points in new directions.
4. Throughout your summary, build toward a climax or point, but don't overclaim. Have a solid answer to the "so what?" of the research; make sure readers know why they might want to learn or even care about what you are doing.

Remember that all summative reviews must deal with clarification or elaboration of definitions that figure centrally in the work proposed. Terms within studies of language, literacy, and multimodalities need clarification; even terms whose meaning may seem obvious benefit from elaboration and refinement of definition. Consider, for example, the importance in any study of bilingual or multilingual speakers of clarifying what is meant by terms such as *translation* or *interpretation*. Certainly, terms such as *embodiment* need definition because of their potential for confusion with everyday uses. Once the summative account of literature reviews reaches completion in the first iteration, generally in the proposal for research, the fieldwork can move forward.

"WHAT REALLY HAPPENS HERE?"

As fieldwork begins, questions shape and reshape themselves in the mind of the researcher. When Brian undertook the fieldwork in Iran that led to *Literacy in Theory and Practice* (Street, 1984), he had a sense of contradictions between sweeping theories of literacy. He also knew what some ethnographers reported from their fieldwork about how reading and writing "actually" happened. Brian describes how this prior knowledge went with him to Iran.

> When I went to Iran in the 1970s to undertake anthropological field research, I did not go to study "literacy," but I found myself living in a mountain village where a great deal of literacy activity was going on. Maybe part of my interest derived from having done my first degree in English literature. I had moved into anthropology because of dissatisfaction with looking only at "texts." I wanted to locate texts with respect to "practices." I attempted to bring English literature together with anthropology through a Ph.D. on "European Representations of Non-European Society in Popular Fiction." I looked at popular stories of adventure in exotic places: the Tarzan stories, Rider Haggard, and John Buchan as popular authors and Rudyard Kipling, D. H. Lawrence, and Joseph Conrad as more established authors. I

arrived in Iran at my field site already excited by the ways that writing and anthropology could be brought together. Perhaps it was this sense that led me to focus closely on the literacy practices of the villagers I lived amongst and even more on the "representations" of these practices by different parties.

I was drawn then to the conceptual and rhetorical issues involved in representing the variety and complexity of literacy activity at a time when my encounter with people outside of the village suggested the dominant representation was of "illiterate" backward villagers. Looking more closely at village life in light of these characterizations, I saw not only a lot of literacy going on but several quite different "practices" associated with literacy—those in a traditional "Quoranic school," those taking place in the new state schools, and the inscribed means that traders used in their buying and selling of fruit to urban markets. Versions of literacy by outside agencies (e.g., state education, UNESCO, and national literacy campaigns) did not capture these complex variations in literacy happening in one small locale where the people were generally characterized as "illiterate."

What happened in Brian's case repeats in certain ways for every ethnographer: A host of questions emerge from initial curiosity about patterns of symbol structures and their uses.

In terms of keeping track of *decision rules* that will surely follow on from initial planning and entry to a field site, we see that Brian's approach and interest rest in his own earlier intellectual background. Decision rules within the field site led him to focus more tightly than expected on the variety and complexity of literary uses by the villagers. The ideas, judgments, and practices from accounts of outsiders also became data. The constant comparative principle behind decision rules led Brian to compare the insider world of the villagers with outsider perspectives on that world.

As Brian moved forward, he compared his own findings with those of other scholars of literacy. He studied the work of anthropologist Jack Goody and many international literacy program developers who held to a theory of the "great divide" between literacy and orality. He checked his own data through these theories and began to develop new ideas.

The theoretical validity of his own work in Iran rests on ongoing negotiation with earlier accounts of literacy as well as research that he found when he returned to England from Iran. Eventually, a new hybrid theoretical position emerged from the testing of empirical data that he terms an "ideological" model of literacy (Street, 1984). Had Brian held to the "great divide" theory that dominated literacy studies before and while he was in the field—he had with him a copy of Goody's classic *Literacy in Traditional Societies* (1968)—and had he taken at face value ideas that outsiders had about the villagers' "illiteracy," he would have interpreted his data merely to confirm these notions.

Ethnographic work is dialogic between existing explanations and judgments (whether held by scholars, outsiders, or insiders) and ongoing data collection and analysis. In this chapter, we consider the instruments and means that ethnographers use to collect and manage data while in the field. These techniques hold regardless of the ethnographer's decision rules or professional identity. All the techniques and strategies of data management apply whether the *unit of analysis* is the individual (Roger in Molly's study), groups (skateboarders in Shirley's work or literacy practices in Brian's research), or institutions of formal education (classroom studies of learning).

The Ethnographer as Instrument

As noted earlier, the ethnographer is the ultimate instrument of fieldwork. Necessary qualities of the best ethnographers (and logically linked to what it takes to be a participant observer) include visual acuity, keen listening skills, tolerance for detail, and capacity to integrate innumerable parts into shifting wholes. In addition, every ethnographer must remain silent and communicate only as appropriate by local norms. Silence and a nonintrusive stance come with difficulty to ethnographers who choose to study sites similar to those in which they have previously played a role. For example, if one has been a cricket player and now wants to do an ethnographic study of a cricket team, neutrality on the smallest of matters may be difficult. Former schoolteachers often find themselves attracted to ethnography and head for classrooms to do their research. Except in unusual circumstances, this choice of field site makes leaving behind value judgments about "good" teaching methods, "bad" curricular materials, or "troublesome" students extremely difficult.

Former teachers-turned-ethnographers must think about the benefits they can gain from undertaking ethnography in learning environments unfamiliar to them. They will find it easier to grow familiar with a "strange" site than to maintain a value-neutral stance within the "familiar" classroom. Every ethnographer has the obligation to reveal to those in the local site (as well as to readers of their published research) relevant prior experience and personal features that mark one's identity. (See, for example, Shirley's Prologue to *Ways with Words* [Heath, 1983/1996b], which makes clear her southern identity and her history of connection with classroom teachers and teaching.)

An ethnographer must also consider level of comfort with technologies of data collection. Choices range widely and include surveys, formal interviews, focus groups, photography, and activity logs along with spatial maps, videorecorders, or audiorecorders. Comfort with any of these will depend on both prior experience and current goals, as well as the values of those involved in the study. For example, Shirley used no videotaping in her fieldwork for *Ways with Words* (Heath 1983/1996b), since when she began the work, residents of the communities in which she worked would not have been at all familiar with such technologies. Ethnographers have to resist selecting means of collecting data simply on the basis of their own negative or positive prior experiences. Ethnographers are often compelled to take up new technologies as well as to lay aside those most familiar.

Highly valuable to ethnographers are several data collection methods not generally thought of as "ethnographic," such as spatial mapping of activities or network analysis. Spatial mapping may be done by members of the group under study; for example, Molly mapped the times and places of Roger's practices during a week or on days when he said "all I did was practice." This work revealed the extent to which Roger viewed "practice" as limited to certain times and spaces, when, in fact, he actually practiced in many different locations and time slots.

Spatial mapping requires no special technical skills. For example, in a study of school reform measures that imposed shortened lunch periods and breaks between classes for a secondary school, ethnographers followed around and mapped and timed movements of a random sample of students to determine where they spent their school day, minute by minute. The focus went to interactional talk and how the new time and space allotments altered students' possibilities of having stretches of conversational talk lasting as long as 2 minutes. Spatial mapping showed that students had to move constantly to meet class schedules; they had no time to sit and talk with friends or to visit with teachers or counselors. Those students who did manage to have at least three occasions of 2-minute stretches of talk on any given day broke school rules and left the campus to do so. The study, along with summaries of research on language development of adolescents, led administrators to alter the next year's classroom layout and schedule. Provided in the new plan were more spaces and times for school club meetings, teacher–student interest groups, and career counseling for small groups who met in a casually furnished lounge. Teacher–student respect and rapport improved; truancy dropped (Heath, Paul-Boehncke, & Wolf, 2007).

Network analysis, a classic tool of sociologists, enables ethnographers to see clearly the social connections of individuals and the clustering of their relationships as well as the density and fragmentation of their linkages. The value of network analysis is that it allows us to quantify the social relationships of individuals with one another as well as with institutions and organizations, thus bringing to light social resources and social capital (Lin, 2001; Lin & Marsden, 1982).

SETTING TIME FRAMES

For every ethnographer, realistic choices related to time and timing rank high among decision rules. Time, both of the ethnographer and within the field site, is one of the most culturally and socially ambiguous features of ethnographic fieldwork. Rhythm of the ethnographer's life and that of the individual or group under study must ground data collection. When is the ethnographer available to observe and record? When is this possible in terms of those under scrutiny? Unlike in earlier years of anthropological fieldwork, ethnographers today less often live among those whose lives they are documenting. As noted earlier, full integration or participation into the "real" life of a particular field site is often impossible. In studying certain community organizations, for example, ethnographers might need to indicate that their observations and recordings will take place only on Mondays and Fridays between 4 P.M. and 10 P.M. when both parents and young people are present. Ethnographers need to make other decisions. To what extent can site visits be planned for only "ordinary" time flow? Will the local site allow ethnographers to observe during intense "nonordinary" times (such as examination period for schools or corporate annual review)?

Ethnographers also collect data by extraction and removal. Their interviews and even their conversations insert themselves as obvious means for taking away language data, information, and opinions from locals. Video and photographic records go away with the ethnographer, as do audiorecordings and field-notes. In a formal education institution, for example, ethnographers, with permission, remove artifacts (such as favors at a dinner for parents, brochures, etc.) and documents (such as enrollment forms, advertisements for school events, etc.). To be sure, locals may attach little value to these items, but the fact remains that ethnographic work is more extractive than other forms of research.

In spite of the extractive nature of ethnographic work, every fieldworker has an obligation to respect and therefore not to disrupt, dislodge, or disturb the environment under study any more than is necessary. Certain decision rules the ethnographer makes at the outset of the work can alter this recommendation.

As Chapter 6 indicates, some ethnographers choose to see their work as *applied* or *action anthropology* and enter their chosen field site to work collaboratively with local individuals or groups with a view to effecting change. We do advise that before undertaking fieldwork, especially that which is collaborative with locals, ethnographers talk openly and fully about matters of propriety, ownership, and limits of revelation. It is not always easy to determine the appropriate individuals with whom to work out these arrangements, but every possible effort to do so should be taken *before* fieldwork begins. Moreover, agreements must be in writing, with those determined to have responsibility for both approval (and rejection) of processes and products of the research signing off and knowing the identity of others who are entering into the agreement at hand. It is essential to describe in detail the eventual ownership of the data, rights of review, and arbitration process should one or another party wish to forbid completion of the work and to halt publication. Setting time limits for each of these processes is critical.

A distinct period should exist in which the ethnographer learns from fieldwork before he or she gives advice to others about either practices or policies. Had Brian gone into the Iranian village in collaboration with a local teacher who worked with outsiders to bring literacy, he might never have recognized the embedded literacy practices. In subsequent collaborative work in townships and rural areas with South African ethnographers, Brian recognized the importance of knowing the local situation before implementing what outsiders viewed as "helpful" programs (see Prinsloo & Breier, 1996). In *Ways with Words* (Heath, 1983/1996b), Shirley distinguished between "ethnographer learning" through extensive fieldwork in communities and "ethnographer doing" in which she worked alongside practitioners inside schools. Her work with teachers came after her time in communities had taught her important local knowledge that enabled her to determine the information that could morally be shared and that which should not be made public.

Ethnographic time scales vary. The classic full year of continuous fieldwork may be more suited to sites that undergo annual agricultural cycles than to the varied conditions in urban and "global" contexts. For many topics, only ethnographic inquiry in multiple sites across different time spans can address research questions and policy issues. Each time scale, however, has the potential to maintain a brand of rigor that bears some kinship with classical ethnographies.

Indeed, the emphasis on "time" in early anthropology was itself a product of contemporary historical circumstances and the constraints on what ethnographers could do and where they could go at that time. (See Chapter 6 for more on this point). Bronislaw Malinowksi, often cited as a father of ethnography, stayed in the Trobriand Islands through an annual cycle because of the outbreak of World War I. He went there intending to do the classic "survey" work familiar to anthropologists at that time. When he could not leave, he made a virtue of necessity, learning local languages and following phases in the natural seasonal cycle. "Natural" cycle is relative to purpose and to life of the entity under study. For example, researchers who study institutions of formal education know they need to work within an academic-year cycle. Ethnographers who study business corporations need to follow fiscal-year calendars. Ethnographers also face the constraint that, increasingly, neither funders nor policymakers will pay or wait for the results of long-term research.

Some researchers advocate ways "to compensate for the lack of extensive time in the field" by advising selection of one of three time modes (Jeffrey & Troman, 2004).

In a "compressed time mode," researchers inhabit a site for brief but intensive periods trying to see everything that is relevant to the participants. This kind of work involves identifying one theme and focusing on it in close detail, or following a theme as it plays out within a compressed time frame, such as a school visit to an outside site or a single inspection of a school.

In the "selective intermittent time mode," researchers spend a longer period of time but use a flexible approach, selecting particular foci and events, such as gender, student–teacher relations, and the curriculum, and dipping in and out of the research site to observe these. Here, the researcher makes clear these themes and the process of continual selection of spatial locations and individuals or roles to be studied. In other words, in laying out the choice to use this particular time mode, the ethnographer is still under the obligation to make clear decision rules for selections planned.

The "recurrent time mode" involves a more formal division of the research into temporal phases, such as sampling the beginnings or ends of term or school celebrations across a cycle. Here the aim is to monitor and compare change over time. Researchers could use some combinations of these modes, and there may be others. The value of this typology is that it draws attention to the time dimension of ethnographic research and forces the researcher to consider the relative strengths and weakness of different time modes and to make related decision rules clear. Such an approach liberates ethnographers from the demands of the full-time anthropologist while also maintaining the goals of rigor and validity.

Determining the Space as "Sample" or "Case"

Every location that an ethnographer chooses exists as both sample and case (cf. Dyson & Genishi, 2005; Ragin & Becker, 1992). Anthropologists have often found themselves subject to criticism from other social scientists or positivist-oriented policymakers for not indicating clearly the nature of their "sample" and the "typicality" of their subjects. Some see this criticism as resulting from a focus on "enumerative induction," while a more appropriate criterion for the work of ethnographers is that of "analytic induction" (Mitchell, 1984).

> An anthropologist using a case study to support an argument shows how general principles deriving from some theoretical orientation manifest themselves in some given set of circumstances. A good case study, therefore, enables the analyst to establish theoretically valid connections between events and phenomena that previously were ineluctable. (Mitchell, 1984, p. 240)

As Brian's fieldwork in Iran evolved, he made connections between local uses of literacy there and other social practices, such as identity, power, and commerce (Street, 1984, especially Chapters 5 and 6). Brian's work emerged as a "telling case," providing an "ideal type" of literacy as social practice—not "ideal" in the normative sense but in the sense in which the social theorist Max Weber spoke of our need to recognize that models used by researchers are heuristics for making sense of complexity (see especially Weber, 1949, pp. 89–93).

From this point of view, ethnographers have to see the ordinary or routine in each field site and thereby identify for analytical exposition "telling" instances of behavior that elucidate, contradict, or expand relationships presented in earlier theories or field studies.

To be sure, the anthropological approach underpins ethnographic work, but it need not define the genre. One aspect of anthropology derives from Todorov's (1988) analysis of the relationship between proximity and distance. Anthropologists privilege their ability to act as a "fish out of water," taking a distant view of local practices. Yet they also give highest credit to colleagues who have immersed themselves in local practices and can think like the "natives." Todorov suggests that the issue is not seeing just the either/or but recognizing the full axis. Fieldworkers distance themselves from their home culture as they come into proximity with an unfamiliar social group. They then become more immersed before distancing themselves from their field site as they return home, drawing near again to their own culture. Many return to their field site, thus repeating the cycle of proximity and distance that becomes a reflex for all such engagement with difference and similarity. The ethnographic imagination (cf. Comaroff & Comaroff, 1992) is founded on this cycle and can be applied in microsituations of engagement and comparison, as well as larger ones, including those where researchers enter and leave sites of learning over a period of time.

Too often, following the ideas of anthropologists in earlier decades, ethnographers today appear to think of "their" field site or phenomenon in proprietary terms. Though human subjects protection rules in the United States and Ethics Committee procedures in the United Kingdom and other nations insist that the specific individual, group, or physical location not be identified, ethnographers need to lay out basic contextual and statistical information, at the very least (Wolcott, 1994, 1999). Such detailing allows not only for comparison with other field studies but also for consideration of the applicability of certain theories or explanations to the site at hand.

For example, in studying a family, neighborhood, community organization, school, or business place, the following descriptors are crucial:

- Age, gender, background, and current status or situation of individual or group members of key focus
- For physical sites, population size and approximate distribution in terms of age, role, gender, and other generic identifiers, as well as local resources (e.g., open spaces or libraries) and historical, topographic, and climatic features likely to explain certain patterns of behavior (but note that revelation of some of these details may too closely identify the actual site and therefore may need to be omitted or simply implied)
- Label(s) that the individual, group, or site gives itself (note that even though pseudonyms must generally be used, these can reveal the spirit of the group's sense of itself—for example, Roadville and Trackton, community names used in *Ways with Words* [Heath, 1983/1996b]). Such labels are especially important if the work is to be done within a geographically

situated community; for example, indicate the general name that local residents use to refer to their space (e.g., a "suburb," "development," "housing estate," etc.)

- Means of access and physical mobility available (for example, for a group of young people, what are their local transportation means? What are the costs and availability and range of functions of uses?)

This kind of encompassing set of descriptors helps other scholars put details of communicative interactions in context. Moreover, such details enable readers of ethnographic research to know whether or not, and if so how, findings from one particular study relate to their own.

Summary

Initial literature reviews help fieldworkers plan their decision rules with an awareness of what it means to work within the fragile ecology of any social system. Only by knowing as much as possible ahead of time and then walking as softly and unobtrusively as possible can ethnographers come to understand the dynamism and inertia at work simultaneously in a social system. To achieve this goal, the self-as-research instrument looks not only outward but also inward.

Molly set decision rules to prepare to collect data about Roger's ways of learning. As she thought about who and what she was as research instrument, she also clarified an agenda for learning with and from Roger. She began by meeting with him several afternoons a week to talk and to observe his practices. Soon, however, she realized that on certain days, especially early in the morning, he spent a lot of time practicing. Moreover, he had a group of other jugglers with whom he sometimes practiced.

Gradually, Molly's initial decision rules expanded her times and spaces for observations. Moreover, as she read more literature, she developed different kinds of questions and knew how to observe closely certain aspects of what Roger referred to as "muscle memory" at work. She also learned to group certain kinds of vocabulary that appeared in his talk: technical terms, references to specific jugglers or programs of juggling Roger watched, and strategies he developed to challenge himself. Decision rules, though laid out initially to organize her own time, emerged in consultation with Roger, who began the study hesitant to talk about his learning. As he warmed to the idea and grew more comfortable talking with Molly, some decisions changed; for example, Molly began to share transcripts with him in order to obtain more detailed explanations of technical points.

Meanwhile, as fieldnotes and transcripts accumulated, Molly wished that she had planned at the outset a "truly" organized way of bringing coherence to the chaos of all she was learning. Each time a conversation or observation seemed to reveal a "breakthrough," Molly worried about how to fit this new insight into the whole. In the next chapter, we take up Molly's concerns—ones experienced by all ethnographers. Though no magic formula will ever exist for making sense of the raw data of fieldwork, we lay out some helpful ideas about the guiding value of continuously refining core questions that frame the ongoing study. We also look at tactics and strategies for managing fieldnotes and conceptual memos once the ethnographer is in the midst of the fieldwork.

CHAPTER 4

Research Questions and Fieldnotes

> Fieldnotes are hard to think and write about: they are a bizarre genre. Simultaneously part of the "doing" of fieldwork and of the "writing" of ethnography, fieldnotes are shaped by two movements: a turning away from academic discourse to join conversations in unfamiliar settings, and a turning back again. (Lederman, 1990, p. 72)

As Molly reflected on her own learning, she saw clearly how she was going to bring focus to her research. She read, listened to Roger, looked more carefully, and decided that setting more guidelines and deadlines for herself would give her the feeling she was moving forward.

> "It's not failing; it's just not practicing enough. People will lose patience after like 10 minutes."

> "[I] knew what it felt like, and [I'd] try to emulate that again."

> "Standing is almost impossible. [I] have to walk to keep up momentum."

Roger kept setting challenges for himself so that he never became too comfortable with his achievements. Molly found purpose and direction for her times of observing and talking with Roger. Now she could focus, plan better use of her time with Roger, and keep in mind the give-and-take of asking and answering questions of herself and her fieldnotes. Molly's conceptual memos became her way of talking to herself and making evident what her findings were as she went along. In this chapter, we move through the footwork of doing ethnographic research. We start with ideas of ways to shape preliminary versions of fieldwork that go into a proposal or grant application. We then move through strategies and tactics of managing fieldnotes and channeling their essence into *conceptual memos* that keep track of what the fieldworker learns from week to week.

RESEARCH QUESTIONS

It may seem surprising for "research questions" to appear after a discussion of field entry, tools, time and space decisions, and your own work as an instance of ethnography. As noted earlier, we believe curiosity lies behind the work of most ethnographers. But curiosity does not transfer smoothly into specific questions. However, looking ahead at the field site, selecting subtopics for literature reviews, setting time frames, and making decisions about how you will operate in the field will bring manageable questions into focus.

Let's look at an example. You have a broad interest in the language socialization that takes place when adults switch roles or jobs, and you want to find a context for studying language and other modalities in this kind of adult language learning. Moreover, you have been drawn into the debates about organic food and the rapid increase in the number of organic farmers in England, Europe, and the United States. You are especially curious about how first-generation organic farm communities break with the past and take on a new identity.

Your plan of work forces you to address questions such as these: Will the study take place on one or more small or large farms and in which geographic region(s)? Will the study be comparative and involve only independent farmers or a collection of farmers who work as part of an agribusiness? Which prior convictions (e.g., as a vegetarian, farmer's daughter, or longtime community gardener) do you bring? What is realistic in terms of your location of residence and physical sites available to you for the study? How will you collect your data (combination of survey, interview, observation only or with some participation)? What do you already know about organic farming, its technical terminology, and the legal rules and definitions of "certified organic" in different markets where farmers might ship their produce?

Careful consideration of matters such as these allow you to locate yourself, refine what you know and need to know, and decide how you can realistically undertake the research that interests you. Research questions that emerge after such an initial self-analysis will be based on considerations of spatial, temporal, role, and data collection processes, as well as both academic and practical literatures that need ongoing review.

But bear in mind that even after you begin fieldwork, demands of your personal life will keep modifying research questions. Think, for example, in the study introduced above, of how time demands of fieldwork can conflict with your family obligations. Once you begin fieldwork, you realize that though more time in the field will be possible in the autumn, the time you planned for winter and spring has to be cut back, and your summer site visits will have to be only intermittent.

Research questions now need to be refined. A focus on the transition from conventional to organic farmer can be accomplished through intensive fieldwork in the autumn season when most farm owners begin implementing their plans for switching from conventional to organic. Refined research questions must reflect a focus on language change during these times of transition. In the autumn months, you will devote your time primarily to fieldnotes, audiotaping, and interviews on site.

While away from the field site, you should examine the multimodalities of documents used to socialize conventional farmers during their transition to organic. Contradictions and disagreements between "official" literatures and the popular press will push you to plan specific areas to discuss later with farmers. Documentary films, promotional materials, and news and feature items in the public press should also supplement your site-based data collection. Targets of focus to be addressed during winter and spring return site visits will emerge. For example, technical, legal, and popular materials on the transition from conventional to organic farming make evident highly specific techniques and reporting processes critical to fulfilling legal requirements for certification. Observations during the autumn show large blocks of time required to respond to these externally imposed demands. How do these tasks fit into the frantic pace demanded in late winter and early spring when ordering seeds, planting, and weeding begin? How did the socialization to the vocabulary involved in technical processes, specific agencies, and bureaucratic procedures carry through in later months of the season?

Be Concise

Every academic knows the importance of saying clearly and concisely what the subject and process of research will be. However, brevity and clarity do not follow easily after literature reviews and considerable absorption in planning data collection. We suggest that every ethnographer try out central questions; ask them of yourself. Then sketch your plan of fieldwork with "critical friends." For example, for the organic farming language socialization project sketched above, friends and family may show interest in central questions stated along the following lines:

Organic farming is on the increase everywhere. In the United States, small farmers in some states are switching in large numbers to organic farming. I'm interested in how they get up to speed on the necessary technicalities in the short autumn period before they have to buy their seeds, plan, prepare the soil, and plant during the winter and spring. I've been able to talk at some length to several farmers in a county in Vermont who want to transition from conventional farming to organic. They say they have no idea what learning to "be organic" is really going to entail. They've agreed that during the autumn, I can go to their meetings, spend a couple of days each week with their families, and learn as much as I can about how they come to think and talk "organic." I want to know what they read, watch, and use as they prepare not only the layout of their gardens or farms but also their business plans. Then I'll go back less frequently in the winter and spring to see what their studying of all processes of turning organic means in their most critical months. Who knows, maybe I'll even find out something that those who are preparing farmers to learn how to become "certified organic" might use to make their teaching and preparation of materials more effective in the long run!

The ethnographer might at various points during such an exposition ask a "critical friend" to comment on the value of the questions, validity of the approach, feasibility of actually "finding out" such things from busy and committed people, and so on. Nonspecialists these days frequently evoke the very questions anthropologists with their newfound reflexivity need to address:

- How do you know they won't just tell you what they think you want to know?
- Aren't you interfering with the data by being on site?
- If it's only one site, how can you make any generalizations?

Such comments from critical friends enable ethnographers to become comfortable about what they truly want to know and can accomplish in the planned research. Ethnography can teach us a lot, but we also need to know its limits and constraints and anticipate how our "findings" might be received.

Disrupt Dichotomies

Ethnographers, particularly those in fields such as education where certain categories and dichotomies have firm standing, need to take special precautions. For example, ethnographers who study institutions of formal education can fall into using dichotomies to delineate sites, styles, and situations of communication use. Most of these fail to acknowledge the cultural nature of human development and ways in which all learners, young and mature, look, listen, imitate, reshape, and transmit within learning environments that they themselves define through their own motivations and needs.

Nowhere is the proactive work of directing one's own learning environments more evident than among those learners positioned on the margins (whether through racial, socioeconomic, age, or linguistic barriers). When we begin to note how much learning goes on in play, for example, we have to question the teacher/student dichotomy that dominates studies that take place within classrooms and schools. Such an approach might miss the deeper cultural processes that take place within other relationships and forms of behavior like play, such as moral reasoning, socialization to competition, strategy development, and interpretation of ambiguities (Goodwin, 1990; Roulleau-Berger, 2003; Sutton-Smith, 1997).

Anthropologists have long warned of the ethnocentric bias that lies behind the dichotomy of *formal/informal*. First is the expectation that adults are those who shape *formal* environments, and all contexts without direction by adults therefore seem to carry the designation of *informal*. This notion is shaped by the centralized focus in Western psychology and sociology (as well as the modernization paradigm) on family and school as the primary learning environments.

Yet increasingly, as we come to gain knowledge about peer socialization and life-span learning, we understand that such dichotomies do not hold and that neither families nor schools today can fully carry out responsibilities traditionally expected. With demands on facts and skills exponentially increasing and instruction time decreasing, schools cannot be the sole providers of technical, interface, and organizational knowledge for future workers/citizens. Moreover, as other labor markets compete for workers with technical and professional knowledge, schools are left with teachers whose expertise cannot keep pace with highly specialized knowledge, especially in rapidly changing fields, such as the sciences.

Morever, school budgets for extracurricular learning opportunities (in arts, sports, etc.) have disappeared or decreased in even the world's wealthiest nations. Thus what used to be regarded as "informal" learning within the space of schools is no longer widely available. In addition, even when after-school provision is available, teachers and assistants or volunteers in these situations generally lack the professional knowledge needed to match student needs for technical know-how. With two-working-parents and single-parent households in Western nations, families have decreasing amounts of time with their young. For the after-school hours of their children, families with disposable incomes turn to "intimate strangers" (e.g., child-care providers, sports and arts coaches, and paid specialized teachers) for lessons or classes ranging from piano to karate to children's theater.

Moreover, peer socialization, generally thought to be highly informal, turns out to follow with close examination, a range of organizational characteristics. Games, as well as spontaneous interactions, can be highly formal, ritualized, and tightly structured, often governed by goals, operational strategies, and rules of correction (e.g., Goodwin, 1990). From the developing world as well as postindustrial societies come thousands of studies of learners who organize themselves for certain occasions, needs, or roles into what outsiders must surely see as formal arrangements. Consider, for example, the tightly ruled world through which groups of the young engage in multiparty video games.

A further expectation shaping the *formal/informal* dichotomy involves spatial arrangements and institutional history. Here again, cross-cultural studies of children and youth from various regions of the world, including postindustrial societies, contradict this view. Formality can mark all kinds of different spaces, as the trend of the past two decades for formal weddings in the park reveal. In these cases, the formality generally reserved for within buildings owned by religious institutions moves outdoors. Similarly, highly informal activities can mark spaces generally reserved only for the most formal of procedures and the embodiment of authority (e.g., scientific research laboratories; cf. Latour & Woolgar, 1986).

Finally, the idea of *informal* implies the absence of direct or verbal instruction and demonstration, while *formal* suggests an authority who instructs verbally from a given body of knowledge and with predictable skills (cf. Henze, 1992). More and more, as all users of the Internet can attest, learners across ages become autodidacts, and dominance of an oral set of directions from a single authority vanishes. Visual and auditory signals (e.g., the computer's bleep that indicates an attempted click is futile), as well as trial and error or observation of another, dominate modes of learning.

The multiplicity of learning sources is characteristic of all contexts where learners are guided primarily by what they themselves believe they want or need to know. We often forget, in the face of the dichotomy of *formal/informal,* how retrieval of random information collected through casual exposure is quickly activated by a current real need. All work on sustained learning in community-based organizations as well as across-the-life-span learning situations indicates such is the case.

Key to such learning is critique based on agreed-upon standards of quality and depth of information. Finding enough information to meet instrumental and immediate goals may be acceptable without critique. However, expert experience and judgment become necessary for sustained learning and advancement. Here, for example, community-based organizations that offer long-term meaningful engagement for young people do their best to enlist adults who are experts in their fields—whether dance, instrumental music, agronomy, or social entrepreneurship. Their interactions with young learners do not match usual notions of "informal" or "formal."

In particular, learning is associated with observation and a real (as distinct from realistic) sense of participation with regard to the intensity of observation, willingness to make efforts, and openness to failure (for cases, see Heath & Smyth, 1999; Maira & Soep, 2005; Rogoff, 2003). These responsibilities include demonstration, verbal instruction, modeling and mentoring roles, judgment by external critics and through comparative experiences, and ongoing advancement and rising in-group challenges. Researching such learning processes and the relationships and meanings associated with them in local situations can be a major contribution of ethnography, whose strength is precisely that it can help us move beyond the simple dichotomies, such as *formal/informal*, which we encounter in popular media and writings about pedagogy.

A final point about the ethnographer's research questions. They must be of such a nature that they can be answered through *empirical* evidence. This dictum rules out questions that center around value judgments, pet beliefs or "theories," and normative terms that have standard usage in other fields. To ask if one set of socialization practices is "better" than another is to rule out application of empirical evidence from ethnographic fieldwork. "Better" for what, for whom, or under which circumstances must be delineated in quantifiable and specifiable terms instead.

To want to "prove" one's "theory" of why something happens the way it does cannot be the motivation for ethnography. The ethnographer studying organic farmers' language socialization cannot set out to "show" that those who undertake such a change are smarter or more civic-minded than conventional farmers. Empirical facts applicable here could include sociodemographic data on highest education level achieved or number of local political offices sought by both kinds of farmers in a certain region. But "proof" of the a priori value judgments noted above would still not be achieved.

FIELDNOTES

The history of social, cultural, and linguistic anthropology resides largely in fieldnotes of individual ethnographers. Collections of such notes make fascinating reading, as do individuals' accounts of just how they recorded ongoing interactions (cf. Sanjek, 1990). Rarely, however, do such accounts indicate the fieldworker's means of grasping while in the midst of collecting data what fieldnotes taken over a specific period of time might mean. We recommend *conceptual memos* for this purpose.

We assume here that ethnographers keep their observations and accounts of interactions in notebooks and supplement these with digital audiorecordings onto their computer. We strongly recommend that after each field visit, ethnographers download their digital recordings and ensure that time, location, and names of interactants are in place for each recording session. We also recommend that, at weekly or other regular intervals, ethnographers review fieldnotes, log recordings, and write *conceptual memos*. Some ethnographers keep their fieldnotes separate from their reflections, projections, and reminders to themselves. Others arrange each page of fieldnotes in several columns, noting logistics in one, fieldnotes in another, and reflective material in another. See below for an example of Brian's fieldnotes from a project on home/school numeracy practices.

Ethnographers studying language and other modes tend to include, at a minimum, the following in their fieldnotes:

1. Running account of events in real time
2. Notable short phrases uttered by interlocutors so that audio- or videorecordings can more easily be coordinated with fieldnotes
3. Changes in audience, routines, rituals, and features of context that co-occur with shifts in language and modes.

Brian, in a field study on mathematics practices at home (Street, Baker, & Tomlin, 2005), used columns for separating straight data from his comments and reflections as he recorded events. His data are reproduced in Table 4.1 just as he recorded them.

Table 4.1. Brian Street's Report on Mountford (Mo) home visits: April 13, 2001. Kerry (in Class 1), Mother (M), Father (F), Teacher (T), and Cathy (age 13). A similar table is published in Street et al., 2005, pp. 185–187. All names are pseudonyms.

1. 11 A.M. Home: M welcomed me into sitting room: M, Kerry and Cathy (aged 13, elder sister, at Uplands school), plus three men—Kerry's F, who drives a truck for the Council (it was parked outside) plus two other workers in their yellow jackets (in their twenties), in 12×12 room. The TV was on, plus a small screen for a play station that Kerry and her sister were playing with. I was not invited to sit down, and all the chairs were full, so I remained standing the whole hour, occasionally kneeling beside Kerry to look at the screen. I gave M our letter, and she said the teacher had already raised the question of our coming, with which she was happy. I explained I might come every few weeks over the next year, and she said fine.	In long street just above school, off main boundary road, not in heart of estate. Preliminary visit to get feel of "home" and signal questions to M for future, e.g., own numeracy memories, e.g., school to home; home num and lit; relation to school. Couldn't take notes so this is from memory immediately afterwards.
2. School to home: M volunteered a worksheet that Mr D had sent home—two pages of word lists that he asked her to work through, asking Kerry to name opposites. I asked if the school sent any numeracy work like this home, but she said no. M commented that school had now made rules that parents couldn't come in, which meant they didn't get to see the teacher except briefly in the playground or at parents' evenings—she had been to one recently where the T had given her the handout. School sends books home for parents to read with children: Kerry keeps dodging this, and T said at parents' evening M must try to get it going again—she agreed to me she will try work goes on in school—Kerry seldom tells her much. Keen for her to do well and keeps saying she is doing OK (elder sister, Cathy, had learning problems and is now at Uplands—Special School. Cathy keeps reminding us that Kerry is only a baby and so can't do tasks that she can . . .)	Reinforces notion of school as focusing more on literacy/language work in relation to home than on numeracy? Or is the home finding this easier to accommodate? Like all carers we have seen, Kerry's parents are eager to support their child's schoolwork, though they are not clear what it involves.
3. Home numeracy practices: calendar on wall (squares with number for each day) with days crossed out: over it was a monthly calendar with a line for each day, and this was Kerry's: she consulted her mother's calendar for the days crossed out and then ticked/crossed that day on her own calendar. A clock in the form of a large wrist watch was on the wall, and Kerry named the numbers that the small and large hands were pointing to. She also watches TV and knows the times of programmes. Relations around numeracy, etc.: M asks Kerry questions for my sake, to confirm claims M has made about her knowledge and interests: presses her a bit but generally Kerry is responsive. Kerry keen to show me her playstation activity, so occasionally checks that I am following (caught between sustaining conversation with M and following/being attentive to Kerry). M keen to help Kerry, e.g., M's description of working through wordsheet with her as an encouraging tutor.	Home numeracy practices—does school recognize and build on these?

Wolcott (2001) and others recommend a similar separation of data from reflections, especially when sharing data among several members of a research team. When actual data can be lined up for the same stretch of time, ethnographers can most easily address questions about patterns, relevant theories, and perceptions of occurrences on a particular day. Members of Brian's team would discuss one another's fieldnotes and pick up reflections from the right-hand column for consideration in future visits.

The mention of the playstation, for instance, raised the question for the team as to how far they should pursue questions associated with new technologies that they frequently encountered in their home visits. In the end, the team decided that, interesting though this topic was, their focus was more precisely on everyday numeracy practices, and they would note computer use only as it related to these. To do otherwise ran the risk of turning the project into a "home computer" study. Such in-the-field decisions relate not only to prior literatures reviewed but also to resource and time constraints. The two-column method of recording data addresses such questions and feeds usefully into the content of conceptual memos.

CONCEPTUAL MEMOS

Written each week in connection with logs of recorded data, *conceptual memos* need not be more than five or six pages. Yet they should be as their title suggests: a memo to the ethnographer about generic ideas that come from particular events, along with queries raised in the reflections column of fieldnotes.

For the sake of efficiency, place the following information in the upper left-hand corner of the first page: name of researcher (especially in collaborative work), dates of period covered by memo, sites included, and primary activities or scenarios observed.

Shirley recommends that three sections follow. Titled "Problems and Setbacks," this first section is especially important in research teams, for it briefly indicates unexpected occurrences (e.g., stolen equipment, death in community, etc.). The second section, entitled "Overview," indicates hours in the field, physical locations, and primary sources of data (e.g., conversations of interactive groups or individual interviews). Entitled "Patterns, Insights, and Breakthroughs," the final section constitutes the heart of the memo. Here the ethnographer hones in on patterns detected, insights or trends, and "aha!" realizations. These should not repeat material from prior memos, for when the ethnographer writes the final product from the research, all these memos will be read as cumulative.

An excerpt from a conceptual memo written by Adelma Roach, one of the ethnographers who worked with Shirley in her long-term study of arts-focused youth organizations, follows:

> Something I observed is the way the staff refers to involvement of the youth. In an article in the *Christian Science Monitor,* James [pseudonym for an older member of organization Adelma was studying] was quoted as saying: "We selected teens we felt could be best served by the program." Another pamphlet about the project highlights how teens will be "empowered" through the work they do. . . . While both statements are accurate and important, I wonder what [name of organization] would say about how the young people themselves actually serve and empower the organization. In other words, what are young people giving to the organization that adults would not? How much room for youth involvement and service to the organization itself is there at all levels of planning and work?

The memo continues with several instances and transcript portions in which the young people adopted roles that changed the dynamics of the current work. Adelma wrote:

One young woman took on the role of "tour guide" in a visit
to one of the work sites of the program, dancing, singing, and
talking. She turned to the group at one point: "You guys coming or what? I'm giving the grand tour here. I had to take in
lots of information to do this." Everyone laughed and followed
on. In another instance, a member of the team was asked
to give a weather report. He adopted the persona of a local
weatherman and led the group into facing what was to be a
hot, humid day through laughter and cheers. . . . The young
people come to life when they give me advice about how I'm
doing and extend the knowledge they've been taught to me
as novice. This process of transfer of information and shift in
relations and positioning is useful in understanding contexts
of learning and the roles of assessment and critique they serve
within the organization.

Ethnographers who maintain their conceptual memos on
a regular basis find that when they plan their final written
report, chapter topics fall into place through a phrase or word
search of conceptual memos. Themes, trends, and insights become chapters and their subheadings in the final dissertation
or book.

Summary

Molly soon realized she was no longer standing still but gaining momentum. With each new occasion of watching Roger
and listening to him, she felt more comfortable, as though she
had caught on to how to turn back to the literature, then to her
fieldnotes and recordings, and then back again to new readings. A breakthrough came when she returned to a chapter on
waitressing (from Rose, 2004) she had read earlier. Unlike waitresses, who strongly identify their role in the specific physical space of their restaurant, shop, or bar, Roger had no such
location reinforcement for his identity. His own body was the
physical space of his identity. This small switch enabled Molly

to zero in on the multiplicity of ways that Roger talked about where and how his body was in space, not only in juggling, but also in walking or doing other daily activities. Every conceptual memo revealed to her how ideas were cohering. Molly became more convinced that the knowledge she was gaining could be useful to others. She began writing, analyzing transcripts and fieldnotes, going back to conceptual memos, returning to literature reviews, and then reviewing sections of her fieldnotes and interviews. The final product was falling into place. Her conceptual memos had mapped the locations of data that now cohered for theory development.

CHAPTER 5

Analysis and Coming Home from the Field

For an ethnographer everything is a matter of one thing leading to another, that to a third, and that to one hardly knows what. (Geertz, 1995, p. 20)

As Molly analyzed her fieldnotes, she kept seeing Geertz's words come true. At one point, in reviewing her conceptual memos, she realized that Roger's comments seemed to grow in contradictions. Her fieldnotes, audiotapes, transcripts, and piles of photographs yielded not one or two reassuring patterns but several. She decided to turn again to more reading of literature reviews, where she picked up ideas related to the back-and-forth nature of learning as well as to the challenge for individuals of settling into their work.

She also realized that the questions she asked Roger at certain points had helped push his meta-framing of juggling actions. Roger's technical descriptors such as "flat pattern on a plane" or "alternating outward passes" came in later talks with him more frequently, along with emotional assessments of his process as "fun," "exciting," or "like a mystery." Sweeping generalizations kept company with tiny details about certain tactics he used.

"I was too excited after I got it to spend the time and actually look up technique."

"Four balls—that I looked up online to get the general pattern . . . and the pattern was much easier because I could comprehend three balls."

83

"I got the idea to use the two chairs off a unicycling website online."

"I met a professional juggler, actually, who worked at the YMCA, and he just gave me some other ideas. After seeing the guy, I got inspired."

As Molly began to analyze her ways of capturing Roger's world of juggling, she experienced feelings ethnographers face as they come to the end of their fieldwork. Shaping a final written product lies in the will to stay balanced between one's own data, ideas from literature reviews, and the conviction that you as ethnographer have a contribution to make.

LANGUAGE IN ACTION

Studies of language, literacy, and multimodalities depend on closely linking patterning of symbol systems with abstract behavioral systems. Transcription, annotated and coordinated with time notations, constitutes the first step toward analysis. However, the key mistake of ethnographers who study language is letting transcription take over. "I'm still transcribing" becomes the excuse for stagnation in final analysis and writing.

Therefore, before any transcribing, ethnographers have to log digital recordings, noting time, place, key speakers, and their primary artifacts. In this initial logging (ideally done within 2 days of each occasion of recording), ethnographers note what at that point seems "ordinary" or "nonordinary" in language, behaviors, and context. Most of the material that ethnographers record digitally and include in their fieldnotes reflects the daily routine in the field site. Yet when ethnographers begin their work, they cannot distinguish between what may be ordinary and what could be norm-breaking or out-of-the-ordinary. Later such distinctions become clearer. The log of the ethnographer's first run-through of digital recordings and reading of fieldnotes provides a memorandum of general contents and points of comparison and contrast. Rereading these logs from time to time and certainly in the write-up stage will reveal how the ethnographer has identified events and behaviors that fit ordinary patterns and those that do not over the course of the fieldwork.

Early logs also narrow the range of topics of key interest. Studies of language and other modalities of communication generally include the following areas of focus: individual and group language development, socialization, identity distinctions; change in structures and uses of modes; discourse and narrative; social theories and language and literacy use. We look below at how to log data in these domains.

Individual and Group Language Development

As ethnographers coordinate logs of ordinary and nonordinary language and events with fieldnotes, developments in terms of both content and structure of certain language and modalities emerge.

Shirley's study of self-chosen learning environments for young people outside formal institutions took place during the 1980s and 1990s, decades of deep public hostility toward adolescents in many Western countries, especially the United States. Television and other media portrayed teens as unable to plan, think ahead, consider others, or weigh the consequences of their actions. Shirley, working with a team of young ethnographers who looked like adolescents but were college-age, first collected data around the public media portrayal of adolescents, particularly those living in underresourced communities. Next they asked questions about the actual learning environments of teens. What was happening in places such as community service organizations, garage bands, arts centers, and sports groups? What patterns of behavior could be seen in their everyday practices of interaction, communication, and production? What kinds of questions did the teens ask? What were they curious about? How did young people use syntactic forms that would reflect scenario building or consideration of multiple variables at work in specific situations? How did they represent levels of affect, reasoning, and assessment about their own situations as well as those of others?

Shirley found in her studies of Little League baseball players that on Monday practices early in the season, players' questions routinely focused on management of logistics: "When can we get water?" "What happens if we're late more than three times?" In the fourth through eighth weeks of the season, questions of more than eight morphemes centered on broad processes of play about one-third of the time and on strategies of players in certain positions the other two-thirds.

Of those questions regarding strategies, however, only by the sixth week did some team members pose their questions as hypotheticals that included various possibilities of outcome depending on how certain plays might work out. This pattern raised the hypothesis that as players practiced more game techniques and talked about strategies, they gained fluency in posing hypothetical scenarios in which several variables could affect decision making.

As the weeks went by, players talked more about their mental images of plays. They asked questions that posited a complex combination of events: "If the short stop catches the fly in the eighth inning with the score tied and a base runner heading home on a steal, then what? (cf. Heath & Langman, 1994).

From data collected on teams in different regional locations, researchers noted repeated instances of unexpected contrasts. Across different types of sports, data showed that hypothetical questions dominated question types later in the season only for those teams in which coaches used videotapes of other games and blackboard sketches of plays. These teams logged more hours watching other players in motion on screen, talking about possible variables, and hearing their coaches lay out different possible plays. Models of language, focused visual observation, and opportunities to work through hypotheticals of multiple variables made for meaningful practice. Multimodal representations of concrete plays correlated with players' developing verbal competence with internalized future scenarios.

Eager to learn the extent to which problem-solving think-ahead language worked for team building, Shirley's research team looked at expressions of empathy and management of emotional setbacks among team members. Shirley's initial log of this tape provides an instance of male teens on one team engaging with "bad news" and asking questions about "delicate" topics. Shirley listened to the recording, noted distinctive grammatical patterns, and reminded herself of a contrasting situation from earlier in the year.

> DIGITAL AUDIO LOG: September 14, 1995 (Tuesday), 4 P.M.: Coaches (both Don and Alan) brief their players on schedule and responsibilities for fieldtrip. About 20 minutes into recording, Martin's mother comes in with news that Ryan (top scorer in last week's game) has been seriously injured in a bike accident on the way to the YMCA. The boys' talk following the news goes for 4½ minutes and is full of varieties of types of questions, expressions of mental state, illustrations of empathy, and scenario development that Manuel and Riley seem to lead. One or the other asks: "Will he be OK? How can we cover for him in today's game?" [TRANSCRIBE (and compare with early summer's similar event when Don's wife lost her baby).]

This log entry notes nonordinary talk, approximate length, and context.

Manuel and Riley, boys the research team had decided early in the season would be "target individuals," had come to the team at the urging of their probation officer, who described the pair as highly uncommunicative risk takers and potential school dropouts. In their response to Ryan's accident, both broke with their usual roles in group conversation. During their 4 months on the team, they had heard their coaches and other team members reinforce one another with positive language, make plans, consider alternatives, and assess outcomes. Yet neither of the boys had previously assumed leadership or asked questions, except those related to procedures (e.g., "What happens if we're late?"). The language development of the boys as individual speakers was being tracked in logs, where Shirley was noted when they expressed genres of empathy, concern, and future scenario thinking. Shirley was especially careful to note in the logs any contributions from either boy that differed from their usual ways of talking in the group.

Relating events, modes, extent of time, uses of language, and styles of coaching meant that Shirley's research team could identify co-occurrences and contrasts for later language development of specific individuals such as Riley and Manuel, as well as the group as a whole. This work raised further hypotheses that asked about the extent to which the language development went with them beyond the playing field or basketball court. Longitudinal comparative analysis showed that members of those teams that offered extensive practice and modeling of the kind of language used in planning ahead and considering consequences gained fluency in the syntactic forms necessary for scenario building. Over a 6-month period, their language with friends in nonsports activities showed a greater increase in the grammatical forms that support hypothetical thinking than did members of teams that did not engage in video reviewing, scenario development, and interaction with coaches that modeled planful language (cf. Heath & Langman, 1994).

Identity Distinctions

Ethnic, academic, or legal labels the public media use for any group under study can easily slide into ethnographers' analysis, unless they use extreme caution about adopting any external labels as "given." For example, more often than not, in learning environments that attract young people, external labels take on different meanings. Teens deconstruct, ignore, invoke, and reshape their identities through shared interests, activities, and joint engagement. How they do this shows up only through close transcription of stretches of language in which they rework stereotypes; position themselves interactionally; and invoke irony, parody, and humor to reveal their ideas about how to create groups and manage boundaries (Rampton, 1995; Reyes, 2007).

Showing interactional work around numerous identities can most efficiently be done during close transcription, analysis, and writing. For example, while writing up a chapter section on how male and female athletes differ in their vocal reactions to disrupted plans, Shirley made a discovery. As the season progressed, members of both male and female teams developed predictable ways of managing daily tensions and inconvenient disruptions of plans (e.g., a flat tire on the van). On these occasions, groups of both genders raised general questions (e.g., "Who's checking out the van before next week's away game?").

On the other hand, when personal tragedies (such as accidents, illness, or death) beyond the control of team members took place, male and female teams differed significantly in terms of the number and intensity of personal questions they asked. Female players layered questions within their own narratives of loss, whereas male players rarely related their personal stories to the entire group. On the rare occasions when Shirley caught such narratives on tape, they took place only with teammates who were friends beyond team membership. Within the team, however, long-term male members twice as often as females used narratives as "evidence" when they were "talking out" an interpersonal problem, such as a perceived racial slur or insult to family (cf. Heath, 1994).

Changes in Structures and Uses of Modes

Throughout fieldwork, to get at patterned ways of talking and using other modalities in relation to co-occurring circumstances, the ethnographer needs to sample short portions for transcribing. Perhaps no element of ethnographic fieldwork that focuses on language is more misunderstood and misused than transcription. We have to approach transcription as "a cultural activity used for creating and sustaining a science of the particular slice of the universe that interests us," which in the case of readers of this volume is likely to be "the role of speaking and other communicative practices [including multimodal literacies] in the constitution of persons and communities" (Duranti, 2006, pp. 308–309). Sampling the materials on audiorecordings helps open our "professional vision" (Goodwin, 1994) to enable us to turn the language and contextual data back and forth iteratively.

For example, for those recordings that Shirley made of young sports teams during practices, she initially transcribed 10 straight minutes 40 minutes into practice for every fifth practice session. Laying these transcriptions next to one another revealed changes in particular language structures and uses and shifts in the roles and types of modalities used. Such a random and detached selection of transcribed material ensures that the ethnographer does not simply select for illustration data that meet or "prove" a pet theory or preconceived idea.

The sampling process described here enables the ethnographer to move beyond this initial comparison of stretches of speech or behavior to attend to particular linguistic features. Those chosen for focus will depend on research questions and the relevance of certain kinds of language uses or structures to other aspects of identity, location, or behaviors. For example, because the public perception of teens so often characterizes them as unable to "think about consequences" or "plan ahead," Shirley paid special attention in her comparison of transcripts to syntactic structures (e.g., *if–then* propositions) and mental state verbs (e.g., *worry, plan*, etc.) that characterized scenario building and planful thinking.

But linguistic features beyond syntactic structures also reflect cognitive and social operations. In every society, repetition, overlap, and interruptions in spoken language index such meanings. Local cultural norms determine the specific meanings that interlocutors may or may not pick up. Studies of gender and language in corporate environments, for example, consistently show that in small-group meetings, males interrupt women more often than women interrupt men. Yet males who review the recordings of such meetings rarely acknowledge any awareness that they could do such a thing on a regular basis. Repeated studies of teachers who claim to "let students do most of the talking" reveal that, when teachers review recordings of their classrooms, they hear themselves interrupting and talking over students (Heath, 1983/1996b). Yet they maintain that their ideology would preclude such behavior on their part. Here transcription shows how far apart the ideal and the manifest can be for all of us: We claim we do one thing in language while others see and hear us do something else entirely.

Careful transcription of spoken language can also show a co-occurring pattern that might never have been predicted. For example, Shirley has shown that among young workers in community organizations, interruptions and overlaps take place frequently, but these tend to be grammatically congruent. That is, young people are "in one another's heads" to such an extent that they can anticipate what another will say and therefore say the same thing at the same time. This level of detail and its co-occurrence with young people's sense of being "on the same wavelength" is useful for revealing social cohesion of a group. In contrast, when such transcripts reveal nongrammatically congruent interruptions and failed sentence completions of another's utterance (often producing the protest "that's not what I was going to say"), it is likely that participants will not report a sense of social cohesion of the group.

The practice of randomly sampling data to search for patterns is nowhere more important than in studies of multilingual and multimodal situations. When and how do speakers select among languages, and in connection with which identifiable co-occurring features of the situations? When and how do other modes, such as video materials, appear in current interactions, get referred to by speakers, or appear as contextual artifacts (e.g., posters of famous players, clothing with logos of favorite teams, etc.)?

Logs that note ordinary and nonordinary stretches of language compare easily with fieldnotes that cover similar periods of time. Such a comparative framing enables ethnographers to detect behaviors that co-occur with certain uses and choices of languages and modes. For example, Shirley found that youth sports teams that include multilingual players tend to use languages other than English among themselves in relation to spatial location (inside a building or out on a playing field), as well as day of week (less use of English after weekends away from practice). In the early weeks of a season, if players brought in or referred to other modes, they drew on televised broadcasts. Later in the season, players tended to expand their modes, bringing in diagrams of plays, newspaper photographs, and so on. The same pattern occurred in arts-focused youth groups. As the year moved forward, young artists reached further away from their usual media (video, television, etc.) to bring new modes (articles on museum exhibitions, advertisements using certain principles of graphic design, etc.) into their talk about art with their peers (Heath & Smyth, 1999).

QUANTITATIVE ANALYSIS

Measures of frequency and duration, of phenomena such as turn exchanges among speakers, can be done by either simple means (such as rank ordering of frequencies in different contexts) or by more complex statistical techniques (such as multinomial logistic regression analysis). (See Chapter 8, LeCompte & Schensul, 1999 for detailed description of ways to manage quantitative data.) Quantification has figured centrally in the work of sociolinguists, lexicographers, historical linguists, and computational linguists. Sociologists, cultural psychologists, and linguistic anthropologists depend on using key quantitative concepts, such as mean, average, frequency, correlation, and regression.

Much of the history of literacy comes from scholars who have analyzed census track data, registries of births and deaths, and library check-out records (Cressy, 1980; Graff, 1979, 1987). Every ethnographer needs some level of competency with statistics. The depth that comes from the ethnographer's in situ longitudinal looking, listening, and recording more vividly becomes the "ideal case" when set beside available quantitative data from other sources, such as census tract data or other national databases. For example, an ethnography of one community-based arts organization benefits from comparative use of surveys and other quantitative data collected on out-of-school opportunities and organizations in communities of similar size. Similarly, case studies or ethnographies of out-of-school learning environments benefit from quantitative analysis of transportation information. In one region, for example, Shirley's research team analyzed bus and train schedules and fares to map differences in extent of access young people from different neighborhoods had to parks, museums, concert venues, and community organizations.

The sampling methods that ethnographers of language use to choose segments for close transcription facilitate quantitative analysis. Rank-ordering, raw enumeration, and regression analyses can deepen meanings and reveal patterns of change over time and contexts for particular structures, genres, or styles of speaking. Counts and categorizations of language structures, uses, and their accompanying artifacts in multiple modes intensify the layering of meaning that should characterize ethnographic writing.

DISCOURSE AND NARRATIVE

Discourse analysis, as well as *narrative analysis,* benefits when ethnographers quantify certain forms in terms of audience, associated artifacts, types of activity, and so on. Discourse analysis enables the ethnographer to search for specific grammatical forms and lexical items. These can be structurally analyzed and related to other events taking place in the environment. Numerous books and websites offer insights on the usefulness of both discourse and narrative analyses and suggest specific techniques of transcription and coding. Many discuss particular software programs and their usefulness in the study of language acquisition, multilingual conversations, or work settings (c.f. Edwards & Lampert, 1993; Schiffrin 1988, 1994; Tannen, 1989).

Each year new software programs for analyzing ethnographic data and language come on the market. Their approaches facilitate search and retrieval and enable correlations of transcribed language with fieldnotes and video materials. Because software programs for analysis change rapidly, we do not give accounts of these programs. We urge, however, that ethnographers consider their own competencies as well as their research questions before choosing software. Be alert to the fact that some programs may exceed both your grasp and your reach. Sophisticated software is not necessary for simple content analysis or word and phrase searches. Even expensive software may do little to help an ethnographer determine length and frequency of exchanges of a particular speaker in interaction with selected other speakers. Software that analyzes ethnographic data primarily provides an efficient means of retrieval and comparison of thematic units. Manipulation and examination of these units in relation to language and other modalities depend on the ethnographer's depth of familiarity with the conceptual content of literature reviews and field data.

Above all, ethnographers must avoid adopting either a software program or an analytic approach before logging a substantial portion of the data. Numerous books on field methods and analysis offer insights on working through fieldnotes and transcripts together (Galman, 2007, offers a true beginner's guide; Sunstein and Chiseri-Strater, 2002, provide examples from studies of reading and writing). Regardless of fundamental sorting or coding processes, when the ethnographer rereads data on a regular basis and also writes and reviews weekly conceptual memos, patterns jump off the page or screen. Specific kinds of discourse and genre analysis can make these cohere.

For example, discourse analysis does not identify genres in reliable ways. Those who use narrative analysis generally follow definitions and methods of certain narrative theorists (such as Michael Bamberg, Jerome Bruner, James Gee, Elinor Ochs, and Stanton Wortham; see also Baynham, 2004; Georgakopoulou, 2003; Inghilleri, 2003). Regardless of analytical technique, however, ethnographers have to see narratives as pointing to the past and the future and use some linguistic sophistication to understand how the Janus-like nature of narratives works in most societies (see Bamberg, 2006; Bruner, 2002; Ochs, 1994; Ochs & Capps, 2001).

Studies of genre derive much from literary and humanistic traditions, and discourse analysts find it difficult to understand how specific genres work without returning to core works in literature, particularly to those examining the history and nature of novels (e.g., Bakhtin, 1965/1984, 1981; Watt, 1957/2001). In general, studies of genre by anthropologists and applied linguists tend to focus on their use within specific settings, such as professions, textbooks, and classrooms (for a review of genre theories and genre analysis in various contexts, see Briggs & Bauman, 1992).

Another influence on the study of discourse comes from historical and current work in rhetoric. Rhetoricians turn to Aristotle as perhaps the first in Western history to discern the strong linkage between certain structures of language and their functions and settings. Much contemporary work on deliberative discourse derives from Aristotle and benefits from philosophical discussions of argument (cf. Toulmin, 1964). Linguists set their work on argument within contexts where particular influences, such as that of the media, work as a backdrop (e.g., Andrews, 2005; Tannen, 1998). Handbooks, how-to manuals, and social histories consider certain genres such as conversation to be particularly sensitive to societal and economic forces (cf. Bazerman, Little, & Chaukin, 2003, on written language; Miller, 2006, on conversation).

The persistent question for those selecting a lens of analysis in the study of language and other modes of communication is: What do I know about the history and definitional debates of this lens I am about to select? Think of the lens as a camera: What are its properties? What can it do? How does it relate to other cameras and other reproductive technologies? Remember that you would not buy a camera simply on the basis of one specific vacation destination. Similarly, do not select an analytic lens on the basis of how it has been used in sites similar to those you are currently studying. Look at the merits of the lenses you choose in terms of the theories that generated them. We highlight here three arenas of theory most relevant in the study of language and other modes of communication: language socialization, social theories, and theories of social change and adaptability, including identity.

LANGUAGE SOCIALIZATION

Linguistic anthropologists have carried out most of the language socialization studies that center on communities and longitudinal comparative work (Heath, 1983/1996b; Kulick, 1992; Langlois, 2004; Schieffelin, 1990; Schieffelin & Ochs, 1986; Zentella, 1997, 2005). A few collections of language socialization studies (e.g., Duff & Hornberger, 2008) bring together work from other disciplines, as do reports of long-term research by psychologists (e.g., Hart & Risley, 1995, 1999) and intensive examinations of family life and language by sociologists (e.g., Lareau, 2003). But, in the main, language socialization, especially that of older children and adolescents, has received relatively little scholarly attention (but cf. Maybin, 2006, especially Chapter 8). Language during adolescence receives attention primarily in terms of slang and special quirks, such as the use of *like* or *you know*. Similarly, studies of the acquisition of bilingualism and multilingualism are in short supply (but see Bayley & Schecter, 2003; Zentella, 1997, 2005).

Research on the later language development of adolescents (such as that called for in academic discourse) tends to take place in the normative frame of school achievement. Relatively few ethnographers focus on the interdependence of reading, writing, and uses of multimodal literacies in adolescents' range of learning environments (such as peer groups, special interest groups, or community organizations, but see Jewitt, 2006; Jewitt & Kress, 2003; Kral, 2007; Kress & Van Leeuwen, 1996, 2001; Rampton, 1995). Studies of multimodal literacies often attend to snapshots of teens' engagements with technologies ranging from video games to mobile phone text-messaging (cf. Flood, Heath, & Lapp, 2007; Leander & Sheehy, 2004). Case studies of individuals or groups mark this research, and few follow-up or transitional studies document specific aspects of lexical or syntactic changes that result from the use of interactive technologies.

The research space of language socialization is therefore wide open for ethnographers, especially those interested in literacy (e.g., Boyarin, 1992; Heller, 1997; Kalman, 1999; Lofty, 1992). We offer in this section a brief review of core issues still in need of the attention of ethnographers. We do so because, so often, ethnographers who set out to study reading and writing never consider their interdependence with oral language. The tight relationship between oral language—particularly in terms of lexical, syntactic, and generic productive skills—and written language (both its interpretation and production) cannot be over estimated. Readers and writers need to be orally fluent in the specialized genres and styles that characterize the literacy demands of institutions, such as schools and courtrooms. For example, without extensive practice in conversation (as well as prior academic experience), students face immense struggles in writing academically appropriate essays (Heath, 1993, 1997b).

Ethnographers need to remember some fundamental aspects of language socialization and learning in all their work.

For example, all language learners can understand language more complex than that which they may produce. Very young children, just before falling asleep, often produce highly complex stretches of language they have overhead during the day (Nelson, 1989; Weir, 1962). Children's literature uses complex language and unfamiliar vocabulary as well as illustrations that amplify textual meanings. Think, for example, of children's picture books, world-class editions of fairy tales, and classic favorite children's books, such as those illustrated by Maurice Sendak. Unlike reading textbooks used in schools, commercially produced literature for children and young adults purposefully includes "advanced" lexical items, syntactic structures, genres, and concepts that young readers are not likely to hear in their everyday oral worlds. Remembering this fundamental can help ethnographers attend closely to the level of oral language input for learners in specific situations (such as classrooms) in contrast to the output (oral and written) required.

Other fundamentals of language socialization can also help ethnographers, especially those studying classrooms, bring to bear literature reviews relevant to specific topics such as nature and extent of teacher and student talk. For example, several bodies of longitudinal research document the fact that in book reading with caregiving adults, young children hear twice as many words per minute as they do in everyday non-literary interactions (Snow, Tabors, Nicholson, & Keuland, 1995). The amount of talk between children and their caregivers makes "meaningful difference" in the course of building a rich repertoire of language (Gopnik & Meltzoff, 1997; Hart & Risley, 1995, 1999; Laureau, 2003). Knowing such points will lead ethnographers to examine measures of complexity, fluency, and interactivity of teacher–student discussions of written materials. Familiarity with the language socialization literature also refines research questions. If an ethnographer's transcripts made in classrooms of students with low achievement levels in reading indicate that the teacher uses simple vocabulary and syntax, talks little about children's literature, and rarely engages in conversational interaction with learners, then comparative attention may need to go to written texts, peer conversations, and media language the students use outside the classroom context.

An additional point from the language socialization literature has special relevance for formal learning situations. Research shows that the success of individuals in academic achievement, professional employment, and civic life tends to correlate with fluency in a wide repertoire of language structures, uses, and modes. Research also suggests that learners acquire such a repertoire most reliably through being able to play meaningful roles that give extensive practice in emotionally supportive environments. In technologically advanced nations, infants, toddlers, and young children learn most of their early language uses and structures through interactions with family members and close family friends or paid day-care providers. For the very young, verbal language ideally comes along with food, loving care, and familiar surroundings (e.g., furniture, pets, toys, books, etc.). No such reward system exists for later language development when students need to achieve competency in academic discourse. Professional development of special language and multimodal needs, such as those of attorneys, engineers, computer scientists, or cartographers, often proceeds most effectively as learners increase their meaningful role engagement. What might this mean for formal learning environments and later language development—that required in academic life, adult learning situations, and new professional identities?

Here the comparative perspective of the ethnographer becomes very useful. Language learners judged ineffective in academic settings in which they can play only one role—that of student—learn complex language outside these settings (cf. Rampton, 1995). Generally, psychologists attribute such differences in learning curves to motivation and interest. Yet ethnographers show that other factors—observable in the learning environment but not within the individual—make a difference. In particular, supportive strict adult models who work alongside learners provide language input that young learners pick up. Playing a variety of "adult" roles that carry real consequences within a situation or organization also ratchets up language performance. The young member guiding guests through youth organizations uses vocabulary and syntax that the role of student does not call for in the same manner. Sports, drama, choirs, dance, and community service offer project-based meaningful learning that depends on developing strategies to identify and solve problems collectively with adults. By opening up adult roles in "real" situations that involve scenario development, hypothetical reasoning, and comparative analysis of problems, learning environments offer critical language practice needed for individuals to gain fluency. Ethnographers need to document the collaborative learning of sports, volunteer work, arts organizations, or religious groups in which learners in middle childhood, adolescence, and young adulthood learn language. Ethnographers can enumerate the number and types of genres the young hear within stretches of time, from multiple speakers, and in connection with other media (cf. Heath & Smyth, 1999).

Language socialization theories enable ethnographers to see deeply into agents, props, contexts, roles, and trajectories of learning. Such theories help ethnographers refine questions in the course of data collection and lead them away from loose generalizations into empirical evidence—quantitative records and longitudinal and comparative cases that will make their findings credible.

For example, the episode noted earlier was only one of many in which boys' sports team members responded to emotionally distressing news. These did not occur routinely, so their rare occurrences have to be analyzed in comparison with the ordinary, highly repetitive flow of language during team practices. Shirley recorded team members' language for months of practice. Once the boys were on the court, the coach maintained a steady stream of reinforcing language: "Keep it up," "Over there," "Heads up, Kevin." For every session, Shirley recorded the number of continuous minutes of such language, along with the frequency, content, and nature of breaks. When one of the coaches blew the whistle and pulled the team to the side of the court, she recorded those sessions as well. Therefore, over the season, she was able to work out the mean and median number of minutes of reinforcing language during on-court practice, changes in frequencies and lengths of breaks for narratives and explanations, and patterns of talk sessions before and after practices. Logs of these distinguishable segments provided quantitative data and brief descriptors of time, language data, and uses of other modes, such as charts, video material, news clippings, and so on. All these types of data were needed for development of findings that could contribute to language socialization theories.

Social Theories of Language and Literacy

Since the 1980s, ethnographers have tended to move across several dominant themes in their preferences for social theories. All theories, in one way or another, are essentially about constraints and the processes and practices that construct, modify, and reproduce these. Human agency in everyday life meets these constraints, whether of structures (economic and social) or identities (based in gender, racial phenotype, linguistic or ethnic membership). For this reason, particularly since the 1970s, anthropologists have centered their studies in *practices*, taking up *practice theory* based in the work of a handful of theorists from other disciplines (cf. Ortner, 2006, for a review of practice theorists). Terms such as *communities of practice* and *literacy practices* have become commonplace in the work of ethnographers.

Anthropologists, more than other social scientists, have been drawn repeatedly to the works of French sociologists and philosophers or British political theorists and sociologists who attempt to understand culture, social structure, identity, subjectivities, and power relations. Some of these theorists, such as Pierre Bourdieu, Michel Foucault, and Anthony Giddens, have consistently dealt with power within the cultural or institutional order and have given special attention to institutional powers that shape language.

Anthropologists with special interests in postcolonialism have benefited from the work of Frantz Fanon, Stuart Hall, Edward Said, and Gayatri Spivak. Studies of language socialization also often reflect the influence of Pierre Bourdieu's writings on *habitus* as well as the works on language input and social class by Basil Bernstein. Long dominant among theorists of literacy and its potential for raising political consciousness has been the work of Paolo Freire. Prominent among theorists who have guided thinking about the philosophy of the social sciences are Jürgen Habermas and Thomas Kuhn.

Scholars who carry out studies of communication with a strong interest in identity often reflect the ideas of Gilles Deleuze on becoming and on understanding difference not on the basis of external factors but through internal temporal processes. Contributors whose work has advanced understanding of gender and race include several North Americans: Judith Butler, Orlando Patterson, and William Julius Wilson. European and North American humanists, such as Roland Barthes, Hayden White, and Henry Louis Gates, have brought numerous contributions from literary and cultural theories to the social sciences.

No book, such as this one, with a central purpose of encouraging deeper thinking about research approaches, can begin to do justice to the range of social theorists whose work matters in the study of language and multimodal literacies. However, we note above a few major theorists and their areas of influence on ethnographers to encourage exploration of theorists beyond those best known within the field of language and literacy studies. As you read below on two areas of keen interest to ethnographers—social literacies and academic literacies—we hope you decide to explore the expansive power of locating these areas of pursuit in the context of social theorists not generally called upon in studies of schooling or of literacy. Those who work in *critical ethnography* in their studies of education reach more widely than other ethnographers, but they depend primarily on North American theorists.

Social Literacies

Definitions of literacy often refer to a distinction between an *autonomous model* and an *ideological model* of literacy (Street, 1984). The *autonomous model* of literacy works from the assumption that literacy in itself, autonomously, will have effects on other social and cognitive practices. From the perspective of social theories of power, this model of literacy disguises the cultural and ideological assumptions and presents literacy's values as neutral and universal. Research in the *social practice* approach challenges this view and suggests that in practice, dominant approaches based on the *autonomous model* are simply imposing Western (or urban) conceptions of literacy onto other cultures through selected institutions.

The alternative *ideological* model of literacy offers a more culturally sensitive view of literacy practices as they vary from one context to another. For these reasons, as well as the failure of many traditional literacy programs (Abadzi, 2003; Street, 2006), practitioners and academic researchers have concluded that the *autonomous model* of literacy, on which many practices and programs are based, has been neither appropriate nor effective. Diverse language uses, social needs, and cultural realities around the world fit better within an *ideological model* (Aikman, 1999; Doronilla, 1996; Heath, 1983/1996b; Hornberger, 2002; Kalman, 1999; King, 1994; Robinson-Pant, 2004; Wagner, 1993).

In order to research literacy as *social practice*, many within this framework have advocated an ethnographic perspective, in contrast to the experimental and often individualistic character of dominant approaches to literacy in both research and policy. Much work in this ethnographic tradition (Barton, Hamilton, & Ivanic, 2000; Collins, 1995; Gee, 1990/1996; Heath, 1983/1996b; Street, 1993a; Street & Hornberger, 2007) focuses on the everyday meanings and uses of literacy in specific cultural contexts and links directly with how we understand the work of literacy programs, which themselves then become subject to ethnographic enquiry (Robinson-Pant, 2004; Rogers, 2005).

Key concepts in the field that facilitate the application of these new conceptions of literacy to specific contexts and practical programs include *literacy events* and *literacy practices*. A *literacy event* can be classified as "any occasion in which a piece of writing is integral to the nature of the participants' interactions and their interpretative processes" (Heath, 1982, p. 93). Brian has employed the phrase *literacy practices* (Street, 1984, p. 1) as a means of focusing upon "the social practices and conceptions of reading and writing," although he later elaborated the term both to take account of events in Shirley's sense and to give greater emphasis to the social models of literacy that participants bring to bear upon those events and that give meaning to them (Street, 1988). Barton, Hamilton, and colleagues at Lancaster University have taken up these concepts and applied them to their own research in ways that have been hugely influential both in the United Kingdom and internationally (cf. Barton, Hamilton, & Ivanic, 2000). Careful delineation of contexts of valuation and use of "dominant" and "nondominant" literacies, as well as *vernacular* and *standard* languages in written forms, become central in the ethnographer's analysis. This means being able to pull from fieldnotes and interviews the who, when, what, where, and how of manifest practices as well as the ideals expressed by users and institutional representatives.

Academic Literacies

One direction of ethnographic studies has been toward researchers' own institution—the university. The field of *academic literacies* has done similar things for the issue of student writing in higher education as the *social literacies* perspective has done in the domains of international development, community literacies, and so on. An *academic literacies* perspective treats reading and writing as *social practices* that vary with context, culture, and genre (Barton & Hamilton, 1998; Street, 1984, 1995). The literacy practices of academic disciplines can be viewed as varied social practices associated with different communities. From the student point of view a dominant feature of academic literacy practices is the requirement to switch writing styles and genres between one setting and another, to deploy a repertoire of literacy practices appropriate to each setting, and to handle the social meanings and identities that each evokes (cf. Ellis, Fox, & Street, 2007).

Building on theories of reading, writing, and literacy as social practices (Barton, 1994; Gee, 1990/1996; Street, 1984, 1995), scholars in New Literacy Studies have argued for a new approach to student writing and literacy in academic contexts that challenges the dominant "deficit" model.

Rather than engaging in debates about "good" or "bad" writing, these ethnographers examine writing in academic contexts, such as university courses, at the level of epistemology. They argue that approaches to student writing and literacy in academic contexts could be conceptualized through three overlapping perspectives or models: (1) a study skills model, (2) an academic socialization model, and (3) an academic literacies model. The three models are associated with particular conceptualizations of both language and learning theory, each having its own associated roots and traditions.

The study skills model is concerned with the use of written language at the surface level and concentrates on teaching students formal features of language, for example, vocabulary, sentence structure, grammar, and punctuation. It pays little attention to context and is implicitly informed by autonomous and additive theories of learning (such as behaviorism) that are concerned with the transmission of knowledge.

In contrast, the academic socialization model recognizes that subject areas and disciplines use different genres and discourses to construct knowledge in particular ways (cf. Berkenkotter & Huckin, 1995). The academic socialization model is associated with the growth in constructivism and situated learning as organizing frames as well as with work in sociolinguistics, discourse analysis, and genre theory.

The academic literacies model draws on both the skills and academic socialization models but goes further than the academic socialization model in paying particular attention to the relationships of power and authority to meaning-making and identity that are implicit in the use of literacy practices within specific institutional settings. Importantly, this approach does not view literacy practices as residing entirely in disciplinary and subject-based communities but examines how literacy practices from other institutions (e.g., government, business, university bureaucracy, etc.) are implicated in what students need to learn and do. Recent work on the "marketing" of higher education, for instance, might be called upon here (cf. Barnett & Griffin, 1997) The academic literacies model is influenced by social and critical linguistics (cf. Fairclough, 1992). This model also benefits from critiques of sociocultural theories (Bloome et al., 2005; Lewis, Enciso, & Moje, 2007) that emphasize a theory of learning that foregrounds power, identity, and agency in the role of language in the learning process.

Studies of academic literacies especially benefit from ethnographic work, because prior work on reading and writing in higher education has centered in prescriptive statements, program descriptions, or quantitative measures of discrete skills. Ethnographers who take higher education venues as field sites will provide a distinct perspective that will facilitate development of new directions in practice theories and advance language socialization by pushing the idea of later language development. Such ethnographers have produced a wealth of rich accounts of academic literacy practices that have contributed to both theory and policy (Ganobcsik-Williams, 2006; Ivanic, 1998; Jones, Street, & Turner, 2000; Lea & Stierer, 1999).

SUMMARY

Molly's dilemma at the outset of this chapter reminds us that those we study, in their actions, beliefs, and words, will never offer up easily discernible patterns. The complexities of human life come through in striking ways when we try to figure out just how individuals and groups learn and how those who teach and model think instruction and socialization work. A focus on language and multiliteracies in learning and teaching will aid refinement of our tasks as we sort complexities, but these symbol systems and their combinations bring their own issues.

As ethnographers, we are never more in the classic hermeneutical circle than when we are working with language data embedded in behavioral contexts. The ethnographer has to work from a seemingly unending circle into a spiral that gradually lifts the ethnographer to a vantage point in which the listening and looking make for clarity of meaning. It is up to the ethnographer to record, sort, rethink, revisit, and reconcile conflicting, nonparallel data and misleading bits and pieces.

In this chapter we have described some ways in which the ethnographer moves beyond initial hunches and curiosity to collect data and develop theoretical frameworks to shape the final written product. We have given some of the nuts and bolts of how to do this, showing that only when the ethnographer knows both what has and has not been researched and set forth as theories can analysis of one's own data move generatively. Brian and Shirley entered their various field sites curious about different aspects of language and literacy. Within their field sites, they refined initial research questions. Brian developed a focus on contrastive frames of practice and valuation around "literacy" and "illiteracy." He asked how past theories could have been so linear and so devoid of attention to literacy practices.

Shirley's early interest in language socialization of children and young people and her literature reviews led her to ask how studies of early language acquisition had so outnumbered those on later language development. She wondered how ethnographers had failed to develop an interest in syntactic structures and types of questions used by adolescents in different kinds of learning environments. For Shirley, such questions jumped out of literature reviews and resulted from simple counts of the number of studies of classrooms in contrast to research on other learning environments.

In this chapter, you have also been introduced to reviews of literature on key theories relevant to the study of language and multimodal literacies in the hope of giving you new insights into your own analysis. As Geertz cautions, ethnographers face the fact that each new thing leads to the next and the next and so on. In the end, the back-and-forth of all these processes must sit firmly in the conviction that you as ethnographer have a contribution to make. You have something to say and empirical data to support your theories, and only you can make clear the decision rules that guided your data collection and analysis toward theoretical contributions. But to get these theories beyond the data, you have to avoid creating your own barriers while in the field and once you are in the writing process for a finished product. Transcriptions can be a huge sinkhole from which you have no idea how to emerge. Failing to log recordings while you collect data can leave you with no coherent idea of what you really are left with at the end of fieldwork. Delaying the writing of weekly conceptual memos will mean that you have no retrievable trail of your own insights and breakthrough ideas while you are in the midst of the fieldwork.

Our suggestions regarding techniques of analysis reiterate what ethnography means for the focal concern of this volume: language and multimodal literacies. Several key areas within this general field need empirical work as well as renewed theoretical work. These include individual and group language development, language socialization, identity distinctions; interdependence of structures and uses of modes; discourse and narrative analysis in the context of learning; and social theories of language and literacy use. We have urged a strong quantitative eye for analysis of data as well as a consistent search for co-occurring features of language uses and structures as metaframes for learning.

When Molly felt overwhelmed and bored by advice and admonitions about techniques of data analysis, she reminded herself of Roger's comments (which we give at the outset of this chapter and the next). Facing final decisions about techniques of analysis, Molly lacked the excitement and will that had taken her through data collection. Like Roger, she had loved the exhilaration that came when she "got it" at various points along the way. But now she listened to her data in new ways to get through this crisis of confidence. She heard Roger's points about having "to spend the time and actually look up technique" and "to see what other people are doing." Knowing that Roger had to figure out what he called "this stuff" on the way to achieving his juggling act gave Molly hope. Now all she had to do was manage to keep her balance in the ethnographer's equivalent of Roger's "slack lining."

We believe you take on these challenges and the "hardly knows what" nature of work in ethnography in more satisfying ways when you know something of the company you join. The next chapter gives a brief and subjective history of ethnography from the perspective of our own particular career trajectories. We hope this history and our points of view will be informative, while they also provide context for what others may believe it means for you to assume the mantle of "ethnographer." We have held off these notes on history until we could help you emerge from the field confident and ready to write and report your work for public scrutiny. We hope you can now look at your own contribution and that of these forerunners as being ever in the embrace of the particular time and place of the fieldwork.

CHAPTER 6

Taking Note of History and Writing Ethnography

So I begin with the unfolding of *this* story, of *this* book: how the shape of experience, the questions I asked and the responses I received, even the writing of the ethnographic text, occupy a space within a particular history of a specific ethnographer and her informants as we sought to understand each other within shifting fields of power and meaning. (Kondo, 1990, p. 8)

By the end of Molly's exploration into ethnography through her study of Roger as juggler, his explanations of what he was doing had moved far away from his early demonstrations and conversations about what he was doing. He now talked about making diagrams, coming to understand center of gravity, and being synchronized. He used terms such as *rotation, timing, parabola, intervals, optimal height,* and *alternating outward passes.* Molly knew that her presence had provoked Roger to think about his work in some different ways. She was grateful that she had both his talk and his demonstrations and flow of practices to help her grasp what all these terms meant in a world of unicycles and balls and in the worlds and words of theories she had read.

"You need to be taught in the beginning to get the pattern down. There's a little bit of knowledge of all this stuff that you have to use."

"It's useful to see what other people are doing even if it doesn't apply to you. Even if it's not working for you, it's just kind of interesting to see how other people are thinking about the task, and that gives you some insight and more understanding about it."

"Your instinct is to go slow, but as you actually start doing it, you figure out that is a really bad idea because you don't have enough momentum."

"The hardest part about slack-lining was actually figuring out how to set up the anchor; that took me a long time because it was just diagrams."

As she learned from Roger, Molly balanced what she saw, heard, and read as she analyzed fieldnotes and worked her data into a theoretical perspective. Her experience and evocation became *theory* "where the binary between 'empirical' and 'theoretical'" (Kondo, 1990, p. 8) no longer seemed to mark strict boundaries.

Molly realized that Roger kept attesting to the value of knowing what other jugglers have done. The same is true for ethnographers. Roger also knew his juggling was not just for himself but also and eventually for the public as well. So was Molly's ethnography.

In previous chapters, we have given advice on preparing for fieldwork, collecting and analyzing data, and working with theoretical frameworks. We now turn briefly to the history of ethnography within anthropology and then to the writing up of field data in this context. We do so because as ethnographers we are all entangled in this past in one way or another, just as we are embedded in the present through our own empirical data. Every *this story* plays out against the backdrop of *those stories* from the history of other ethnographers in other times and places.

THE EMBRACE OF ANTHROPOLOGY

Ethnography as a written genre originally resulted from accounts that anthropologists gave of long-term fieldwork—referred to as "doing ethnography," generally in other societies. From its beginnings, this genre has come in response to an incalculable combination of individual bravado, turns of fortune, and felt needs, whether of nation-states, academic networks, explorers, or reformers. Ethnography is now claimed and referred to in the work of many disciplines, but we begin with a brief account of its use in British and U.S. anthropology.

The British Scene

Ethnography has a specific history in British intellectual traditions, and this section briefly recounts the goals and methods that have emerged in the past century. Contests over these, often in subtle ways, continue to underpin aspects of current usage of ethnographic methods.

Social anthropologists in Britain have a well-defined myth of ancestry that gives a key role to both doing and writing ethnography. We noted in an earlier chapter the story of Bronislaw Malinowski, a Polish émigré who went to the Trobriand Islands to do social surveys (Goody, 1995; Kuper, 1996, 2005). Because he was caught there when World War I broke out, his long-term fieldwork became an imposed "choice." When Malinowski returned to the United Kingdom, he promoted long-term residence as the way to learn "native" ways of thought. He then proceeded to write a number of celebrated ethnographies about the Trobriand Islanders, their sexual customs, economic systems, and beliefs (e.g., Malinowski, 1922). He obtained a lecturing post at the London School of Economics and became a founding father of modern British social anthropology. Nineteenth-century anthropologists had worked mostly through surveys that either they themselves conducted or, in the case of Sir James Frazer, compiled from accounts by travelers, missionaries, and district commissioners who corresponded with him. Malinowski's experience became the basis for extended ethnographic fieldwork in social anthropology. His students from the London School of Economics, such as Sir E. E. Evans-Pritchard, Meyer Fortes, Max Gluckman, Edmund Leach, and Lucy Mair founded Departments of Anthropology in Oxford, Cambridge, and Manchester, and their ethnographic accounts of African and Asian societies in particular became the scholarly groundwork on which future generations of anthropologists have built (Kuper, 1996).

Those working in this tradition had to learn local languages, adapt to local customs of finding and preparing food, and gain substantial knowledge of how others lived and thought. Such long periods of separation from their own culture, as well as the inevitable questioning of ingrained attitudes of their own cultural superiority, led many early ethnographers to reveal as much about themselves in their writings as about those whose lives they were attempting to record. Languages, political systems, religion, gender relations, and means of warfare figured centrally as topics of first concern in ethnographies written by European and British scholars (Jacobson, 1991; Kuper, 2005).

Then and now, anthropologists' interests link closely with contemporary economic and national self-interests and cannot be thought of as simply a detached academic pursuit. From Malinowski's day forward, ethnographic work has never been far away from economic and political special interests. Particularly in the history of anthropology in Europe and especially in England, ethnographers had close relations with government. Their relationship was, indeed, dialogic. Universities and branches of governments could (and often did) give logistical and intellectual support to explorations and residencies that resulted in ethnographies, new cartographic versions of distant lands, and refined estimates of the life of natural resources. Anthropologists often thought of themselves as challenging the colonial powers and in some way helping to insulate "their" people from the misunderstandings of a central imperialist authority (cf. Lienhardt, 1964). Recent debates in British and European anthropology recall these "engagements" and wonder why there seem to be fewer of them today (Eriksen, 2006; Kuper, 1999, 2005). In other words, why is it that policymakers turn so rarely to the work of ethnographers? (For an analysis of why this may be the case, see Hammersley, 1992).

The American Scene

By the early 20th century, North American academics began to recognize a critical need for the work of anthropologists and linguists (Darnell, 2001; Segal & Yanagisako, 2005; Stocking, 1974, 1992). Indigenous populations in North America were shrinking in number, and with the loss of each group, languages, ecological wisdom, and patterns of living were disappearing forever. Major figures such as Franz Boas of Columbia University promoted collection of word lists, details of written symbols, and speech genres as a way of "salvaging" these "disappearing worlds." Others offered historical recounts and details of contemporary conditions for the last survivors of certain tribes.

These anthropologists recognized that indigenous populations possessed critical knowledge of their regions as well as a historical understanding of human migration. These histories shaped views of land ownership and use of natural resources that could prove vital to environmental sustainability. Anthropologists and linguists feared loss of this indigenous wisdom with the death of the few remaining survivors of certain tribes or the last speakers of Native American languages. Their anthropological sense often clashed, however, with the values and goals of individual expansionists, timber and mining developers, and engineers and politicians behind the spread of transport networks. Moreover, many indigenous groups, remembering deceptions and treacheries of the past, had grave reservations about sharing information with outsiders. The fieldwork, publications, and professional conventions of anthropologists and linguists remained almost entirely within academic circles.

With the world wars, however, the U.S. Office of War Information and Foreign Service recognized the value of anthropologists and linguists in understanding "alien enemies." By the early 1940s, the government was sending anthropologists and linguists all over the world to learn local languages and record fieldnotes. In addition, ethnographers collected artifacts of daily life as well as locally generated maps and any quantitative records of production and use of regional resources. All of these, as well as surveys and time-task analyses, enabled ethnographers to bring together the local patterns of daily life and language in specific times and places.

Support of social science work by U.S. governmental agencies began in the 1940s and continued through the 1950s. Well-known figures in the history of American anthropology and linguistics not only worked in Japan, New Guinea, Samoa, and the Solomon Islands, but they also set up language schools, surveyed language situations, and documented the ways of speaking, acting, and believing in parts of the Caribbean, Middle East, Indonesia, and India. Names such as Conrad Arensberg, Gregory Bateson, Ruth Benedict, Charles Ferguson, Clifford Geertz, John Gumperz, Dorothy Lee, Margaret Mead, and John and Beatrice Whiting appear in governmental reports, and their work sometimes led to local and national support of linguistic and anthropological study. Simply recording numbers of individuals and elements of the environments provided no basis for deep cultural and linguistic understanding or for taking in the kinds of learning necessary for adapting to coexistence. Ethnographers could fill this gap by offering descriptions and analyses of language, life ways, and patterns of belief. These could inform governments and their emissaries about the range of social, ideological, and cultural differences spread across the world. Anthropologists' accounts of these "patterns of cultures" became the first relatively widely read ethnographies in the United States. (See especially Benedict, 1934/1959, with a Preface by Margaret Mead, and publications of the American Ethnological Society during the 1930s; other exemplars include Bateson, 1936; Bateson & Mead, 1942; Mead, 1930, 1956.)

In the decade following World War II, the United States turned from military conflicts to exploration in distant territories for natural resources and military base locations. As the Cold War and the "Red scare" moved upward on the scale of American fears, military representatives were sent to locations of both cultural and climatic extremes. Climates such as those of Alaska, the Antarctic, and arid deserts presented physical and navigational challenges for which American military personnel were not prepared. In the 1950s, U.S. gains in scientific research compared poorly with the advances being made in the Soviet Union. This realization, along with acknowledgment of the lack of foreign-language expertise among Americans, led to establishment of the National Defense Education Act (NDEA), supporting foreign-language programs and accelerating scientific research. These governmental initiatives renewed recognition of the work of linguists in particular.

By the second decade after World War II, however, governmental interest in anthropology and linguistics waned except in response to immediate crises that forced attention to language and culture differences. Then governmental support through funding, training, and agency cooperation came through for a short while. Following the Vietnam War, for instance, and the entry into the United States of thousands of refugees from Southeast Asia, some support went to groups, such as the Center for Applied Linguistics, that operated orientation camps for refugees.

This experience with refugees in large numbers and with highly visible phenotypical and linguistic differences led some U.S. policymakers to see a growing need to learn more about these peoples and cultures. Educators found it difficult to handle the fact that many immigrants had little experience with written language, institutions of formal education, or the institutional power of literacy of the kind drawn upon in American schools. In communities receiving large numbers of Southeast Asian refugees, religious and sociocivic groups stepped forward to learn about the diversities of regional, ideological, and moral values that the refugees might reflect.

In the 1960s and 1970s, several other national events provided the imperative for seeing, accepting, and learning with and about differences within the U.S. population and in nations around the world. Legal and political acceleration of desegregation stimulated the extensive geographic movement of African Americans. Moreover, European Americans, especially college students active in the civil rights movement, worked and often settled in regions and communities vastly different from those of their early childhood. Enlistment in the Peace Corps accelerated among young college graduates, bringing them into intensive study of foreign languages and direct long-term experience living in faraway lands. The Cuban Missile Crisis, struggles over the status of Puerto Rico, and the rapid increase in the number of political and economic refugees from the Caribbean and the Philippines dramatically altered old neighborhood identities. By the end of the 1970s, services provided by health industries, restaurant and hotel businesses, and janitorial and sanitation companies rested primarily on the labor of recent immigrants.

These face-to-face experiences with cultural and linguistic differences brought a wide array of reactions in Europe and the United States. Entrenched racist attitudes threw up economic and social stumbling blocks for newcomers as well as for African Americans in the United States and long-settled minorities in the United Kingdom, Australia, and elsewhere. In spite of monumental legal decisions after the 1960s, racism went underground to find its way into loan rejections, refusals of housing in certain communities, and uneven provisions of transport, as well as health and education resources. Dozens of personal accounts, along with ethnographies, biographies, and reformist histories, made clear the need and desire to help Eurocentric populations face new sociodemographic realities in many parts of the world (Rogers, 2005).

These current realities, along with the long-standing acknowledgment that ethnography has always worked in the context of such shaping forces, frame the work of today's ethnographers. Ultimately, it is the "company" ethnography keeps that matters, for all social science work must rest on the "accumulated structural knowledge of social life" (Hymes, 1996, p. 13) that goes beyond what any one person can see, hear, record, and analyze. Ethnographers must therefore give due credit to building their work on the shoulders of those that have gone before. From this history, ethnographers should realize that prior field research, as well as their own, has been shaped by contemporary political and economic pressures from governments, funding agencies, and review panels.

Nevertheless, many ethnographers hold dearly to the view that among all the social science methodologies, those that go into the creation of "an ethnography" represent the most democratic and theory-generative. Anthropologist Dell Hymes (1996) described ethnography as "peculiarly appropriate to a democratic society" that would:

> see ethnography as a general possession, although differentially cultivated. At one pole would be a certain number of persons trained in ethnography as a profession. At the other pole would be the general population, respected (on this view of ethnography) as having a knowledge of their worlds, intricate and subtle in many ways (consider the intricacy and subtlety of any normal person's knowledge of language), and as having necessarily come to this knowledge by a process ethnographic in character. In between—and one would seek to make this middle group as nearly coextensive with the whole as possible—would be those able to combine some disciplined understanding of ethnographic inquiry with the pursuit of their vocation, whatever that might be. (p. 14)

These ideas have special relevance for those who undertake applied anthropology in education, medicine, and other service-oriented fields.

Here we consider first the borderland of "applied" research that created boundary problems for anthropologists. We then consider uses of ethnography in education.

Applied Anthropology

The label *applied anthropology* came to prominence in the 1940s when anthropologists in the United States named this subfield to describe their involvement in programs of social change directed toward Native Americans. Many of these studies were done by anthropologists who had worked among Native Americans and had come to recognize the disruptive force of schools and health services run by the Bureau of Indian Affairs (e.g., Wax, 1971; Spindler & Spindler, 1970). Intentions behind this work related to concerns that schools and other institutions imposed by governmental bureaucracies ignored social, religious, and cultural norms of Native American children and their families and therefore ensured isolation and endangered their futures. The work of many in applied anthropology and the anthropology of education attempted to bring to bear anthropological research in order to entice educators and other change agents into awareness of the socialization contexts and local needs of Native American children and their families (e.g., Philips, 1972, 1983).

Applied anthropology also supported the idea that governmental, educational, and medical entities would always need increasing information to understand technology, environmental resources, and issues surrounding "diversity." Whether in the installation of water purification systems in Latin America or promotion of the use of the plow rather than bullocks in farming, applied anthropologists believed that information gained through long-term anthropological studies could benefit programs carried out in the name of "modernization" as well as "diversification" and resource management.

Numerous accounts and assessments of both the efforts of anthropologists of education and those in applied anthropology evaluate the processes and effectiveness of this work (e.g., Lassiter et al., 2005; Segal & Yanagisako, 2005). Critiques center on applied anthropologists' lack of relevant technical knowledge and their naive rush to "help others." Today a majority of anthropologists contend that only when applied anthropology gave rise after the 1960s to specific further sub-subfields, such as medical anthropology, did the necessary interdisciplinarity and technical training come about. For example, when those undertaking research in medical anthropology know a great deal about *both* the medical field and anthropology, their chances of effective work increase. Departments of medical anthropology have come about, and medical anthropologists today tend to have advanced degrees in either public health or a subfield of medicine as well as training in anthropology.

This need for a balance of discipline-based knowledge and clinical and technical know-how becomes especially complex, however, in the case of ethnography in education and even more complicated for the study of language and multimodal literacies in relation to formal education. Until the late 1980s, most individuals in the United States who termed themselves "anthropologists of education" had training in both anthropology and education, though not always with equivalency in both fields. Moreover, most of those working in language and literacy as anthropologists of education also had some training in linguistics (often through sociolinguistics or a four-field approach to anthropology that included linguistics). With regard to language and literacy, David Barton, John Baugh, Niko Besnier, Frederick Erickson, Mary Hamilton, Dell Hymes, Ray McDermott, Susan Philips, Elinor Ochs, Ben Rampton, and Bambi Schieffelin, as well as both authors of this book, reflect such training.

ETHNOGRAPHY IN EDUCATION

Because many readers of this volume will have a keen interest in ethnographic research in education (primarily in field sites of formal schooling), we consider some critical points related to the study of language and multimodalities in this arena. A seminal statement on ethnography in education notes three possible takes: doing ethnography, adopting an ethnographic perspective, or using ethnographic tools (Green & Bloome,

1997). As one might expect, the three reflect greater to lesser degrees of orientation to theories from anthropology.

1. Doing ethnography includes "the framing, conceptualizing, conducting, interpreting, writing, and reporting associated with a broad, in-depth, and long-term study of a social or cultural group, meeting the criteria for doing ethnography as framed within a discipline or field."

2. Adopting an ethnographic perspective means "that it is possible to take a more focused approach (i.e., do less than a comprehensive ethnography) to study particular aspects of everyday life and cultural practices of a social group. Central to an ethnographic perspective is the use of theories of culture and inquiry practices derived from anthropology or sociology to guide the research." (Note that we might add sources of theories, such as cultural studies, sociolinguistics, learning sciences, and, of course, education itself as a field.)

3. Using ethnographic tools such as interviews, time-activity charts, document content analysis, and digital sound recording, allows for "the use of methods and techniques usually associated with fieldwork. These methods may or may not be guided by cultural theories or questions about the social life of group members" (all quotes from Green & Bloome, 1997, p. 183).

Beyond this trio is the critical distinction to be made between ethnographic studies *of* education and ethnographic studies *in* education (Green & Bloome, 1997, p. 186). The first refers to research that results when social scientists study the places and processes that locals consider as involving education (with a small *e*), socialization, or learning. These studies link theories and methods from specific bodies of work in the social sciences through each step of the research: from establishment of research questions to data collection through analysis and integration of past research with new theory development. For example, research on language learning in multiparty interactions might take an ethnographic perspective; go on over a long period of time; and depend on bodies of literature from psychology, linguistics, and anthropology (cf. Blum-Kulka & Snow, 2002).

In the United States, the United Kingdom, and Australia, ethnographic studies *in* education tend to focus on Education with a capital *E*. Scholars who undertake this research generally have a background of teaching or being administrators within primary or secondary schools or institutions of further and higher education. Their study is often motivated by a desire to bring the knowledge gained in higher education to bear on reforming education policies, the school as an institution, specific subject-matter curricula, or pedagogical approaches of individual teachers (for more on these points, see Hammersley, 1992, Chapter 8, and Hammersley, 2006). These individuals typically enroll in graduate schools of education and almost never complete the same sequence of coursework as that undertaken by doctoral students in Anthropology or Linguistics Departments. Moreover, they undertake instead a series of courses that introduce statistical methods, "qualitative" methods, and others dedicated to specialized methods extracted from other fields (e.g., discourse analysis, multivariate analysis, etc.).

They then may choose to use ethnographic perspectives and methods as education researchers, not as anthropologists or linguists, in the sense that their primary focus stems from educational issues and needs rather than from an interest in advancing or testing theories of learning or socialization based in either anthropology or linguistics.

Reflexivity

Anthropologists bear the burden of a discipline that emerged in strong association with colonial and expansionist powers. The doing of ethnography depends on both scholarly and political power. In critiques of the field (e.g., Asad, 1973; Clifford & Marcus, 1986; Segal & Yanagisako, 2005), this association raises tough issues for the validity and value of ethnography and of anthropology as "science." If an ethnographer is identified with a colonizing power or institution promoting inequities of opportunity, then how does this alliance affect responses to questions and the behavior of informants and the observed? And if anthropologists see their work as somehow "emancipating" those they study from oppression, do they not have unrealistic expectations of research as well as naive politics? Clearly, anthropologists with such goals (or even lesser versions of this idea, such as collaboration to "prove" one reading method "better" than another for a school or classroom) cannot claim their data will be "objective." But are the data even valid in the sense of offering a record "true" to principles of the social life among those living and working in the field site? Critiques on these points from within anthropology have been sharp and trenchant. In the end, however, they have left the discipline intact in that the very "reflexivity" that these discussions engender can then be built into preparation for fieldwork and indeed become an endemic part of the study of ethnography in anthropology and linguistics or in fields such as education that engage in "applied" or "practitioner" ethnography (cf. Levinson & Holland, 1996).

Reflexivity, a process by which ethnographers reveal their self-perceptions, methodological setbacks, and mental states, often includes broad general critiques of the field. Reflexivity enables ethnographers to see their research within historical and structural constraints that result from asymmetrical power distributions. Foley (2002) considers reflexivity to be of four types: confessional, theoretical, interpersonal, and deconstructive.

"Confessional" probably captures what most people outside anthropology imagine reflexivity to be—an admission of guilt over the colonial roots of the discipline. Foley takes this position further by considering a range of perspectives that situate the ethnographer, including the more agonistic ones as well as the more balanced "situational" perspectives or autoethnography. Graduate students undertaking ethnography

are often expected, for instance, to lay out something of
the autobiography of both the project and its author and
to indicate how these affected the framing, data collection,
and findings. Often this expectation is set forth as something
new, when, in fact, such has consistently been the case in
ethnographies based on long-term fieldwork (e.g., Prologue
of Heath, 1983/1996b, and summation on this point in the
chapter entitled "On Ethnographic Validity" in Sanjek, 1990).

A less visible type of reflexivity is what Foley terms "theoretical reflexivity," referring to the kind of demand that Pierre
Bourdieu, a French sociologist, put on his colleagues. Bourdieu insisted that his colleagues make explicit the theoretical
bases of their claims, providing a kind of sociology of sociology. For the ethnographer, this demands a loss of "empiri-
cist innocence"; that is, whatever they saw in the field and
whatever they say about it in their writing will be rooted in
theoretical assumptions that need to be made explicit. Most
anthropologists would take these points as crucial to "doing
ethnography."

In education, such reflexivity is perhaps less the norm but
becoming so, as the accounts cited above by Green and Bloome
(1997) and Jeffrey and Troman (2004) make clear. The rhetorical use of representational practices evident in this kind of
reflexivity also points in the direction of another type. "Inter-
textual reflexivity" refers primarily to historical accounts that
locate the data not in a supposedly overarching "ethnographic
present" but instead in a developing and moving "past" (Foley, 2002). Ethnographers have tended to valorize the present.
Consequently, they need the comparison with historians to
help put their claims into perspective and to indicate the importance of narrative style in the construction of ethnographic
knowledge. Some well-known critiques of traditional ethnography rest on their failure to link historical realities with findings from contemporary fieldwork (Clifford & Marcus, 1986).
Such critiques also call on ethnographers to reflect on their
writing process as well as their selected methods of collecting
and analyzing data.

Finally, Foley (2002) refers to the "deconstructive turn" in the social sciences that appears to lay open everything to critique and question and to challenge the foundations of any research paradigm. Foley and indeed most anthropologists greet this position, along with those of "cultural studies," with skepticism. They accept the need to be self-critical as well as well informed on the history of deconstructionism and related critiques of ethnography. (For more on these debates, see Chapters 6 and 7 of Kuper, 1999.) Yet they also present strong arguments for the particular merits of ethnographers' combination of methods and commitment to comparative and long-term positioning.

Foley's (2002) own position is "eclectic," blending the first three kinds of reflexivity and drawing on "highly accessible, highly reflexive realist cultural critiques" and using "all the varieties of reflexivity in practice" (p. 489). We still, he concludes, can only speak as mortals from various historical, culture-bound standpoints. Our claims are inevitably limited and partial. But perhaps by making these limits more apparent and by knowing well what constitutes ethnographic validity, we will make our narrative and analysis more, not less, believable.

All forms of reflexivity as well as the history of the development of ethnography in and of education throw up a challenge that takes us well beyond the earliest postcolonial critiques of anthropology. Today anthropologists and ethnographers in particular work increasingly *with* those they study and share findings along the way. They try to stay alert to the fact that institutions and individuals in power may well use the ethnographer's findings to confirm stereotypes, set policies, or determine critical matters, such as land boundaries and ownership. Ethnographers have to keep learning how to be responsible and sensitive to these possibilities while also using empirical data to answer the question "what's happening here?" We therefore have to take account of limitations and constraints while continuing to advance our understanding of universals of human life and learning. Ultimately, we do so primarily through our writing.

The Making of Public Texts

Considerable pressure exists currently in the United Kingdom and elsewhere for anthropologists to make their work accessible to the public. As ethnographers undertake this challenge, they have to present their data and theories in straightforward ways, making "the world simpler and more complex at the same time" (Eriksen, 2006, p. 130). Ethnographers face a special difficulty in this task, for so often they study and reveal what everyone else may think they already know; this is especially true when ethnographers study people (like Roger) in the process of learning and knowing (cf. Chaiklin & Lave, 1993). Moreover, many in the fields of advertising, marketing, and product development currently undertake methods they term "ethnographic," laying out how people make decisions, communicate, and interact.

In the end, however, ethnographers can set themselves apart from writers who must make their living in the world of commodities and rapidly emerging news events, fads, and niche markets (see Johnson, 2005, for an analysis of "ethnographers as spies" in the marketplace). Ethnographers derive their worth from the integrity and thoroughness of their literature reviews, the constant-comparative and co-occurrence framing of their data collection, and their theory building. In their writing they must, while providing accessible text, make these features of their work clear.

Within anthropology, there is no shortage of excellent guides to writing (cf. Van Maanen, 1988), and we choose here to point to these and to underscore processes of writing that we see as most critical in the study of language and multimodal literacies. Three classics in the field of writing ethnography stand out as handbooks for every ethnographer: Clifford and Marcus (1986), Rosaldo (1993), and Sanjek (1990). Classic models of ethnographic writing, such as that of Clifford Geertz, receive considerable attention in these works. A highly useful plea for "engaging anthropology" in the public mind comes from Eriksen (2006), along with many pointers for the unique benefits that come from ethnographic fieldwork.

To these sources, we would add the following special notes for presenting studies of language and other modes in the making of meaning.

1. Give transcribed material identity with the speaker(s). Consider the work of novelists who enable readers to know the character as well as to hear the words he or she speaks.

2. Locate language and modes in use within their scene, situation, and time frame, remembering always to indicate whether or not episodes are ordinary or nonordinary and what their relative frequency and duration are.

3. Place language segments and descriptions of uses and structures of modes in your text in such a way that readers will see change across scenes, communicators, audience, and time.

4. Weave in and out of your own periods of writing some quiet time for reading fiction and other genres of writing that leave you with details living in your memory. Pay attention to how others write the images or fragments of language you remember. While you were in your field site, your job as ethnographer was to observe details that no one else might notice. As writer you must bring these details to authenticity in the eye, ear, and imagination of your readers.

5. As you write about language and other modes, remember that you are presenting observations of events, words, and moves that you have analyzed and now offer as revelatory signals of patterns that build theories.

6. As you write your theories, weave their parts as a comprehensible grid of narrow streets, not as one wide boulevard that begins nowhere in particular and ends somewhere off in the horizon. In the reader's mind, the streets of your grid should come alive through the data you have collected, analyzed, and represented. Make your theories maps for the explorations of others.

Finally, we offer advice that every handbook of writing suggests as well.

7. Write through your entire work as fully as you can without going back to the first few pages to edit and correct. Write as much as you possibly can before you begin to revise. Most of us think through writing. The more we write, the more we think, and the more we read our own writing, the more both our thinking and our composition improve. As you write, even your first draft, section your ideas into chapters to which you give titles; draw heavily on your conceptual memos, for they often provide many of your chapter titles and themes. Make a table of contents early—even before leaving the field—and always create the cartography and the basic description of your field site before you say good-bye to fieldwork.

Once you have written, rewritten, edited, and edited again, ask some friends who are not in your field to dedicate an hour or so to reading your work. Then invite them for dinner or a long walk and have them tell you what they think you have said. Remember that just as in your field observations your goal was to see what no one else would notice and hear what no one else would detect, so in your writing, your effort should be to open to others what they might have never realized they could know or think.

Summary

The 21st century raises tough questions that require approaches to ethnography that differ in many, but not all, ways from those of earlier anthropologists. Yet we contend that the past matters, for in vital ways, today's ethnography can benefit from knowing yesterday's history of anthropology and the hazards of claims about inside knowledge of "others." Partnership for research, publication, and debate of policies and practices brings into play the respect that ethnographers have often set as a fundamental of their work. These features come along with the ethnographer's "company" of constant comparison, decision rules, and reflexivity to help ensure standards and trust for any particular ethnography. We urge ethnographers to be alert not only to the history of anthropology and the anthropology of education but also to contemporary uses of terms such as "ethnographic" in other disciplines and the public realm. Within the broad arena of applied anthropology, ethnography has a special role to play by documenting how social change institutions influence the choices and chances the young face as they grow into adult members of their societies.

Few events under the big circus tent look smoother and easier than the juggling act of the unicyclist working back and forth on a slack-line. Some might say the same of the apparent ease of observing, participating, listening, and asking that enables ethnographers to create their final showpiece—an ethnography. But perception rarely matches reality in such complex tasks; making the results look easy is all part of the challenge for Roger as juggler and Molly as ethnographer. Both depend on constant attention to skillful balancing, theory building, and "autocorrecting." Both put highly technical and complex concepts into action. Both depend on creating illusions, knowing when there can be "no crossing," and figuring out how to keep going after setting up "the anchor."

Suggestions for Further Reading

Aware of the range of studies using the label "ethnography," we select a few book-length studies here that reflect features of ethnographic work we have highlighted in this volume. Those included here result from extended fieldwork, make decision rules clear, use data to support claims, and establish themselves in relation to theories. Since numerous listings of ethnographies of formal schooling exist, we slant this list toward studies of language and literacy in other learning environments.

Barton, D., & Hamilton, M. (1998). *Local literacies*. London: Routledge.

> Based on ethnographic fieldwork on everyday literacy practices in the Lancaster, England, area, this was one of the first studies in the United Kingdom to apply a social practice perspective to literacy.

Fishman, A. (1988). *Amish literacy: What and how it means*. Portsmouth, NH: Heinemann.

> Early exemplar of a teacher-as-ethnographer struggling to understand her dual role in a world of unfamiliar norms. The work shows how the author intensifies her data analysis as she brings theories of reading to her students.

Gregory, E., & Williams, A. (2000). *City literacies: Learning to read across generations and cultures*. London: Routledge.

> Combines historical and contemporary accounts of the everyday lives of people living in two contrasting areas of London—Spitalfields and the City. Presents a study of living, learning, and reading as these activities take place in pubic settings and the home, calling upon memories elicited from over 50 people. The authors contextualize the accounts and, in so doing, they help dispel dominant myths about literacy in urban multicultural areas.

Heller, C. E. (1997). *Until we are strong together: Women writers in the tenderloin*. New York: Teachers College Press.

> A unique story of an ethnographer as a co-creator of the site she studies. This work sensitively balances reflexivity as "I witness, I feel" and empirical data from adult women writers taking part in a writing workshop.

Kalman, J. (1999). *Writing on the plaza: Mediated literacy practices among scribes and clients in Mexico City.* Cresskill, NJ: Hampton Press.
A study of street scribes and ways their uses of written language established and maintained social relationships. A central contribution of this work is its location of oral language within the technologies and social knowledge involved in writing the loves, needs, and complaints of others.

Kral, I. (2007). *Writing words–right way; Literacy and social practice in the Ngaanyatjarra world.* Unpublished doctoral dissertation, Australian National University, Canberra, Australia.
A detailed PhD study across three generations of Aboriginal people as they moved into closer contact with White Australians. Particularly interesting for linking historical data analysis with ethnographic fieldwork and for the account of contemporary Aboriginal youths' use of new internet technologies in telling their stories.

Lofty, J. (1992). *Time to write: The influence of time and culture on learning to write.* Albany: State University of New York Press.
Rare example of longitudinal fieldwork with students in grades 1, 2, 6, and 12 in a remote geographic site where school-defined literacy seems out of place. Compelling in its uses of multiyear data from the same group of young people, this work demonstrates how maturation influences changes in children's theories about language and literacy.

Prinsloo, M., & Breier, M. (Eds.). (1996). *Social uses of literacy: Theory and practice in contemporary South Africa.* Amsterdam: John Benjamins.
Reports on a number of case studies based on fieldwork in the Cape Town area among different ethnic groups and in rural and urban settings. The study also links ethnography to policy issues in education by showing what it can mean to teach adults how to use literacy to access what they need in their lives rather than to manage decontextualized formalized school-like skills.

Robinson-Pant, A. (2001). *"Why eat green cucumbers at the time of dying?": Women's literacy and development in Nepal. Hamburg:* UNESCO Institute for Education.
A classic ethnographic field study in Nepal. The author collected data by walking many miles across mountain tracks to compare the different ways in which villagers engaged with literacy. As centralized programs penetrated deeper into the hinterland, many people responded to literacy opportunities as irrelevant to the realities of their lives—like eating green cucumbers at the time of dying.

References

Abadzi, H. (2003). *Improving adult literacy outcomes*. Washington, DC: World Bank.

Agar, M. (1996). *The professional stranger: An informal introduction to ethnography* (2nd ed.). New York: Academic Press. (Original work published 1980)

Aikman, S. (1999). *Intercultural education and literacy: An ethnographic study of indigenous knowledge and learning in the Peruvian Amazon*. Amsterdam: John Benjamins.

Andrews, R. (2005). Models of argumentation in educational discourse. *Text, 55*(1),107–127.

Asad, T. (1973). *Anthropology and the colonial encounter*. London: Ithaca Press.

Bakhtin, M. M. (1981). *The dialogic imagination*. Austin: University of Texas Press.

Bakhtin, M. M. (1984). *Rabelais and his world* (Helene Iswolsky, Trans.). Bloomington: Indiana University Press. (Originally published 1965)

Bamberg, M. (Ed.). (2006). Narrative—State of the art [Special issue]. *Narrative Inquiry, 16* (1).

Barnett, R., & Griffin, A. (Eds.). (1997). *The end of knowledge in higher education*. London: Institute of Education.

Barton, D. (1994). *Literacy: An introduction to the ecology of written language*. Oxford: Blackwell.

Barton, D., & Hamilton, M. (1998). *Local literacies*. London: Routledge.

Barton, D., Hamilton, M., & Ivanic, R. (Eds.). (2000). *Situated literacies: Reading and writing in context*. London: Routledge.

Barton, D., & Tusting, K. (Eds.). (2005). *Beyond communities of practice: Language, power and social context*. Cambridge, UK: Cambridge University Press.

Bateson, G. (1936). *Naven: A survey of the problems suggested by a composite picture of the culture of a New Guinea tribe drawn from three points of view*. Cambridge, UK: Cambridge University Press.

Bateson, G., & Mead, M. (1942). *Balinese character: A photographic analysis*. New York: New York Academy of Sciences.

Bayley, R., & Schecter, S. R. (Eds.). (2003). *Language socialization in bilingual and multilingual societies*. Clevedon, UK: Multilingual Matters.

Bazerman, C., Little, J., & Chaukin, T. (2003). The production of information for genred activity spaces: Informational motives. *Written Communication, 20*, 455–477.

Baynham, M. (2004). Narrative in time and space: Beyond "backdrop" accounts of narrative orientation. *Narrative Inquiry, 13*(2), 347–366.

Benedict, R. (1959). *Patterns of culture.* New York: New American Library. (Original work published 1934; 1959 edition contains introduction by Margaret Mead)

Berkenkotter, C., & Huckin, T. (1995). *Genre knowledge in disciplinary communication.* Mahwah, NJ: Erlbaum.

Bloome, D., Carter, S., Christian, B., Otto, S., & Shuart-Faris, N. (2005). *Discourse analysis and the study of classroom language and literacy events: A microethnographic approach.* Mahwah, NJ: Erlbaum.

Blum-Kulka, S., & Snow, C. E. (2002). *Talking to adults: The contribution of multiparty discourse to language acquisition.* Mahwah, NJ: Erlbaum.

Bourdieu, P. (1991). *Language and symbolic power.* Oxford: Polity Press.

Bourdieu, P., & Passeron, J.-C. (1977). *Reproduction: In education, society and culture* (R. Nice, Trans.). Beverly Hills: Sage.

Boyarin, J. (Ed.). (1992). *The ethnography of reading.* Berkeley: University of California Press.

Briggs, C. L., & Bauman, R. (1992). Genre, intertextuality, and social power. *Journal of Linguistic Anthropology, 2,* 131–172.

Bruner, J. (2002). *Making stories: Law, literature, life.* New York: Farrar, Straus, & Giroux.

Chaiklin, E., & Lave, J. (Eds.). (1993). *Understanding practice: perspectives on activity in context.* Cambridge, UK: Cambridge University Press.

Clifford, J., & Marcus, G. (Eds.). (1986). *Writing culture: The poetics and politics of ethnography.* Berkeley: University of California Press.

Collins, J. (1995). Literacy and literacies. *Annual Review of Anthropology, 24,* 75–93.

Comaroff, J., & Comaroff, J. (1992). *Ethnography and the historical imagination.* Boulder, CO: Westview.

Cope, B., & Kalantzis, M. (2000). *Multiliteracies: Literacy learning and the design of social futures.* London: Routledge.

Cressy, D. (1980). *Literacy and the social order: Reading and writing in Tudor and Stuart England.* Cambridge, UK: Cambridge University Press.

Darnell, R. (2001). *Invisible genealogies: A history of Americanist anthropology.* Omaha: University of Nebraska Press.

Dobbert, M. L., & Kurth-Schai, R. (1992). Systematic ethnography: Toward an evolutionary science of education and culture. In M. D. LeCompte, W. L. Millroy, & J. Preissle (Eds.), *The handbook of qualitative research in education* (pp. 93–159). San Diego, CA: Academic Press.

Doronilla, M. L. (1996). *Landscapes of literacy: An ethnographic study of functional literacy in marginal Philippine communities.* Hamburg, Germany: UNESCO Institute for Education.

Dourish, P. (2001). *Where the action is: The foundations of embodied interaction.* Cambridge, MA: MIT Press.

Duff, P., & Hornberger, N. (2008). Language socialization. In the *Encyclopedia of education* (Vol. 8). Hamburg, Germany: Springer.

Duranti, A. (Ed.). (2001). *Linguistic anthropology: A reader.* London: Blackwell.

Duranti, A. (Ed.). (2004). *A companion to linguistic anthropology.* London: Blackwell.

Duranti, A. (2006). Transcripts, like shadows on a wall. *Mind, Culture, and Activity, 13*(4), 301–310.

Dyson, A. H., & Genishi, C. (2005). *On the case: Approaches to language and literacy research.* New York: Teachers College Press.

Edwards, J. A., & Lampert, M. D. (Eds.). (1993). *Talking data: Transcription and coding in discourse research.* Hillsdale, NJ: Erlbaum.

Eglash, R., Bennett, A., O'Donnell, C., Jennings, S., & Cintorino, M. (2006). Culturally situated design tools: Ethnocomputing from field site to classroom. *American Anthropologist, 108*(2),347–362.

Eickelcamp, U. (1999). *Don't ask for stories: The women from Ernabella and their art.* Canberra, Australia: Aboriginal Studies Press.

Eisenhart, M. A., & Finkel, E. (1998). *Women's science: Learning and succeeding from the margins.* Chicago: University of Chicago Press.

Eisenhart, M. A., & Howe, K. R. (1992). Validity in educational research. In M. D. LeCompte, W. L. Millroy, & J. Preissle (Eds.), *The handbook of qualitative research in education* (pp. 643–680). San Diego, CA: Academic Press.

Ellis, V., Fox, C., & Street, B. (2007). *Why English? Rethinking English in school.* London: Continuum.

Eriksen, T. H. (2006). *Engaging anthropology: The case for a public presence.* Oxford: Berg.

Fairclough, N. (1992). *Discourse and social change.* Cambridge, UK: Polity Press.

Flood, J., Heath, S. B., & Lapp, D. (2007). *Handbook of research on teaching literacy through the communicative and visual arts* (Vol. 2). New York: Routledge.

Foley, D. (2002). Critical ethnography: The reflexive turn. *Qualitative Studies in Education, 15*(5),469–490.

Galman, S. C. (2007). *Shane, the lone ethnographer.* Lanham, MD: Altamira Press. [A graphic "novel"]

Ganobcsik-Williams, L. (Ed.). (2006). *Teaching academic writing in UK higher education: Theories, practices and models.* Balingstoke, UK: Palgrave Macmillan.

Gee, J. (1996). *Social linguistics and literacies: Ideology in discourse.* London: Falmer. (Original work published 1990)

Gee, J. (2000). The new literacy studies: From "socially situated" to the work of the social. In D. Barton, M. Hamilton, & R. Ivanic (Eds.), *Situated literacies: Reading and writing in context* (pp. 180–191). London: Routledge.

Gee, J., Hull, G., & Lankshear, C. (1996). *The new work order: Behind the language of the new capitalism.* London: Allen & Unwin.

Geertz, C. (1973). *The interpretation of cultures.* New York: Basic Books.

Geertz, C. (1995). *After the fact: Two countries, four decades, one anthropologist.* Cambridge, MA: Harvard University Press.

Geertz, C. (2005). Commentary. In R. A. Shweder & B. Good (Eds.), *Clifford Geertz by his colleagues* (pp. 108–124). Chicago: University of Chicago Press.

Georgakopoulou, A. (2003). Looking back when looking ahead: Adolescents' identity management in narrative practices. In J. Androutsopoulos & A. Georgakopoulou (Eds.), *Discourse constructions of youth identities* (pp. 75–91). Amsterdam/Philadelphia: John Benjamins.

Gibbs, R. W. (2006). *Embodiment and cognitive science.* New York: Cambridge University Press.

Gladwin, T. (1970). *East is a big bird: Navigation and logic on Puluwat Atoll.* Cambridge, MA: Harvard University Press.

Goodwin, C. (1994). Professional vision. *American Anthropologist, 96,* 606–633.

Goodwin, M. (1990). *He-said-she-said: Talk as social organization among Black children.* Bloomington: Indiana University Press.

Goody, J. (1968). (Ed.). *Literacy in traditional societies.* Cambridge, UK: Cambridge University Press.

Goody, J. (1995). *The expansive moment: Anthropology in Britain and Africa 1918–1970.* Cambridge, UK: Cambridge University Press.

Gopnik, A., & Meltzoff, A. N. (1997). *Words, thoughts, and theories.* Cambridge, MA: MIT Press.

Graff, H. J. (1979). *The literacy myth: Literacy and social structure in the nineteenth-century city.* New York: Academic Press.

Graff, H. J. (Ed.). (1987). *The legacies of literacy: Continuities and contradictions in Western culture and society.* Bloomington: Indiana University Press.

Green, J., & Bloome, D. (1997). Ethnography and ethnographers of and in education: A situated perspective. In J. Flood, S. B. Heath, & D. Lapp (Eds.), *Handbook of research on teaching literacy through the communicative and visual arts* (pp. 181–202). New York: Macmillan.

Greenfield, P. (2004). *Weaving generations together: Evolving creativity in the Maya of Chiapas.* Santa Fe, NM: School of American Research.

Hammersley, M. (1992). *What's wrong with ethnography?* London: Routledge.

Hammersley, M. (2006). Ethnography: Problems and prospects. *Ethnography and Education, 1*(1), 3–14.

Hammersley, M., & Atkinson, P. (1995). *Ethnography: Principles in practice* (2nd ed.). London: Routledge.

Hannerz, U. (2003). *Foreign news: Exploring the world of foreign correspondents.* Chicago: University of Chicago Press.

Hart, B., & Risley, T. (1995). *Meaningful differences in the everyday experience of young American children.* Baltimore: Paul H. Brooks.

Hart, B., & Risley, T. (1999). *The social world of children: Learning to talk.* Baltimore: Paul H. Brooks.

Heath, S. B. (1982). Protean shapes in literacy events: Ever-shifting oral and literate traditions. In D. Tannen (Ed.), *Spoken and written language: Exploring orality and literacy* (pp. 91–118). Norwood, NJ: Ablex.

Heath, S. B. (1993). Rethinking the sense of the past: The essay as legacy of the epigram. In L. Odell (Ed.), *Theory and practice in the teaching of writing: Rethinking the discipline* (pp. 105–131). Carbondale: Southern Illinois University Press.

Heath, S. B. (1994). Stories as ways of acting together. In A. H. Dyson & C. Genishi (Eds.), *The need for story: Cultural diversity in classroom and community* (pp. 206–220). Champaign, IL: National Council of Teachers of English.

Heath, S. B. (1996a). Ruling places: Adaptation in development by inner-city youth. In R. Shweder, R. Jessor, & A. Colby (Eds.), *Ethnographic in approaches to the study of human development* (pp. 225–251). Chicago, IL: Chicago University Press.

Heath, S. B. (1996b). *Ways with words: Language, life, and work in communities and classrooms.* Cambridge, UK: Cambridge University Press. (Original work published 1983)

Heath, S. B. (1997a). Child's play or finding the ephemera of home. In M. Hilton, M. Styles, & V. Watson (Eds.), *Opening the nursery door: Reading, writing and childhood 1600–1900* (pp. 17–31). London: Routledge.

Heath, S. B. (1997b). The essay in English: Readers and writers in dialogue. In Macovski, M. (Ed.), *Dialogue and critical discourse: Language culture, critical theory* (pp. 195–214). New York: Oxford University Press.

Heath, S. B. (2006). Child's play for private and public Life. In E. Arizpe, E. & M. Styles (Eds.), *Reading lessons from the eighteenth century: Mothers, children, and texts* (pp. 179–207). Lichfield, UK: Pied Piper Press.

Heath, S. B., & Langman, J. (1994). Shared thinking and the register of coaching. In D. Biber & E. Finegan (Eds.), *Sociolinguistic perspectives on register* (pp. 82–104). Oxford: Oxford University Press.

Heath, S. B., Paul-Boehncke, E., & Wolf, S. (2007). *Made for each other: Creatives sciences and arts in the secondary school.* London: Creative Partnerships.

Heath, S. B., & Smyth, L. (1999). *Artshow: Youth and community development.* Washington, DC: Partners for Livable Communities.

Heller, C. E. (1997). *Until we are strong together: Women writers in the tenderloin.* New York: Teachers College Press.

Henze, R. (1992). *Informal teaching and learning: A study of everyday cognition in a Greek community.* Mahwah, NJ: Erlbaum.

Holland, D., & Eisenhart, M. (1990). *Educated in romance: Women, achievement, and college culture.* Chicago: University of Chicago Press.

Holland, D., Skinner, D., Lachiotte, W., & Cain, C. (1998). *Identity and agency in cultural worlds.* Cambridge MA: Harvard University Press.

Hornberger, N. (Ed.). (2002). *The continua of biliteracy: A framework for educational policy, research and practice in multiple settings.* Clevedon, UK: Multilingual Matters.

Hull, G., & Schultz, K. (2002). *School's out: Bridging out-of-school literacies with classroom practice.* New York: Teachers College Press.

Hutchins, E. (1995). *Cognition in the wild.* Cambridge, MA: MIT Press.

Hymes, D. (1962). The ethnography of speaking. In T. Gladwin & W. Sturtevant (Eds.), *Anthropology and human behavior* (pp. 15–53). Washington, DC: Anthropological Society of Washington.

Hymes, D. (1964a). Introduction: Toward ethnographies of communication. In J. J. Gumperz & D. Hymes (Eds.), *The ethnography of communication* (pp. 1–34). Washington, DC: American Anthropological Association.

Hymes, D. (Ed.). (1964b). *Language in culture and society: A reader in linguistics and anthropology.* New York: Harper & Row.

Hymes, D. (1974). *Foundations in sociolinguistics: An ethnographic approach.* Philadelphia: University of Pennsylvania Press.

Hymes, D. (1994). Toward ethnographies of communication. In J. Maybin (Ed.), *Language and literacy in social practice* (pp. 10–19). London: Open University Press.

Hymes, D. (1996). Narrative thinking and storytelling rights: A folklorist's clue to a critique of education. In D. Hymes (Ed.), *Ethnography, linguistics, narrative inequality: Towards an understanding of voice* (pp. 109–120). London: Taylor & Francis.

Inghilleri, M. (2003). Habitus, field and discourse: Interpreting as a socially-situated activity. *International journal of translation studies, 15*(2), 243–268.

Ivanic, R. (1998). *Writing and identity.* Amsterdam: John Benjamins.

Jackson, J. (1990). "I am a fieldnote": Fieldnotes as a symbol of professional identity. In R. Sanjek (Ed.), *Fieldnotes: The makings of anthropology* (pp. 3–33). Ithaca, NY: Cornell University Press.

Jacobson, D. (1991). *Reading ethnography.* Albany: State University of New York Press.

Jeffrey, B., & Troman, G. (2004). Time for ethnography. *British Educational Research Journal, 30*(4), 535–548.

Jewitt, C. (2006). *Technology, literacy and learning: A multimodal approach.* London: Routledge.

Jewitt, C., & Kress, G. (Eds.). (2003). *Multimodal literacy.* New York: Peter Lang.

Johnson, R. (2005). Ethnographers as spies. *Sunday Times Colour Supplement.* NP.

Jones, C., Street, B., & Turner, J. (2000). *Student writing in the university: Cultural and epistemological issues.* Amsterdam: John Benjamins.

Kalman, J. (1999). *Writing on the plaza: Mediated literacy practices among scribes and clients in Mexico City.* Cresskill, NJ: Hampton Press.

King, L. (1994). *Roots of identity: Language and literacy in Mexico.* Stanford, CA: Stanford University Press.

Kondo, D. K. (1990). *Crafting selves: Power, gender, and discourses of identity in a Japanese workplace.* Chicago: University of Chicago Press.

Kral, I. (2007). *Writing words—Right way: Literacy and social practice in the Ngaanyatjarra world.* Unpublished doctoral dissertation, Australian National University, Canberra.

Kress, G., & Street, B. (2006). Foreword to K. Pahl & J. Rowsell (Eds.), *Travel notes from the new literacy studies: Case studies in practice* (pp. vii–x). Clevedon, UK: Multilingual Matters.

Kress. G., & Van Leeuwen, T. (1996). *Reading images: The grammar of visual design.* London: Routledge.

Kress, G., & Van Leeuwen, T. (2001). *Multimodal discourse: The modes and media of contemporary communication.* London: Arnold.

Kulick, D. (1992). *Language shift and cultural reproduction: Socialization, self, and syncretism in a Papua New Guinean village.* Cambridge, UK: Cambridge University Press.

Kuper, A. (1996). *Anthropology and anthropologists: The modern British school* (3rd ed.). London: Routledge.

Kuper, A. (1999). *Culture: The anthropologists' account.* Cambridge, MA: Harvard University Press.

Kuper, A. (2005). Alternative histories of British social anthropology. *Social Anthropology, 13*(1), 47–64.

Langlois, A. (2004). *Alive and kicking: Areyonga teenage Pitjantjatjara.* Canberra, Australia: Pacific Linguistics, Research School of Pacific and Asian Studies, Australian National University.

Lankshear, C. (1997). *Changing literacies.* Buckingham, UK: Open University Press.

Lankshear, C., & Knoble, M. (2003). *New literacies: Changing knowledge and classroom learning.* Philadelphia: Open University Press.

Lareau, A. (2003). *Unequal childhoods: Class, race, and family life.* Berkeley: University of California Press.

Lassiter, L., Cook, S., Field, L., Sjoerd, R., Peacock, J., Rose, D., & Street, B. (2005). Collaborative ethnography and public anthropology. *Current Anthropology, 46,* 83–106.

Latour, B., & Woolgar, S. (1986). *Laboratory life: The construction of scientific facts.* Princeton, NJ: Princeton University Press.

Lea, M., & Stierer, B. (Eds.) (1999). *New contexts for student writing in higher education.* Buckingham, UK: Open University Press/Higher Education Research Association.

Lea, M. & Street, B. (1997). Student writing and faculty feedback in higher education: An academic literacies approach. *Studies in Higher Education, 23*(2), 157–172.

Leander, K., & Sheehy M. (2004). *Spatializing literacy research and practice.* Bern, Switzerland: Peter Lang.

LeCompte, M. D., & Schensul, J. J. (1999). *Analyzing and interpreting ethnographic data.* Walnut Creek, CA: Altamira.

Lederman, R. (1990). Pretexts for ethnography: On reading fieldnotes. In R. Sanjek (Ed.), *Fieldnotes: The makings of anthropology* (pp. 71–91). Ithaca, NY: Cornell University Press.

Leung, C. (2005). Convivial communication: Recontextualising communicative competence. *International Journal of Applied Linguistics, 15*(2), 119–144.

Levinson, B., & Holland, D. (1996). The cultural production of the educated person: An introduction. In B. Levinson, D. Foley, & D. Holland (Eds.), *The cultural production of the educated person: Critical ethnographies of schooling and local practice.* Albany: State University of New York Press.

Lewis, C., Enciso, P., & Moje, E. (Eds.). (2007). *Identity, agency and power: Reframing sociocultural research on literacy.* Mahwah, NJ: Erlbaum.

Lienhardt, R. G. (1964). *Social anthropology.* Oxford: Oxford University Press.

Lin, N. (2001). *Social capital.* Cambridge, UK: Cambridge University Press.

Lin, N., & Marsden, P. V. (Eds.). (1982). *Social structure and network analysis.* Beverly Hills, CA: Sage.

Lofty, J. S. (1992). *Time to write: The influence of time and culture on learning to write.* Albany: State University of New York Press.

Luke, A., & Carrington, V. (2002). Globalisation, literacy, curriculum practice. In R. Fisher, G. Brooks, & M. Lewis (Eds.), *Raising standards in literacy* (pp.246–260). London: Routledge.

Maira, S., & Soep, E. (2005). *Youthscapes: The popular, the national, the global.* Philadelphia: University of Pennsylvania Press.

Malinowski, B. (1922). *Argonauts of the western Pacific.* New York: Dutton.

Marcus, G. E. (1995). Ethnography in/of the world system: The emergence of multi-sited ethnography. *Annual Review of Anthropology, 24*, 95–117.

Marcus, G. E. (1998). *Ethnography through thick and thin.* Princeton, NJ: Princeton University Press.

Maybin, J. (2006). *Children's voices: Talk, knowledge and identity.* Basingstoke, UK: Palgrave Macmillan.

Mead, M. (1930). *Growing up in New Guinea.* New York: Dell.

Mead, M. (1956). *New lives for old: Cultural transformation—Manus, 1928–1953.* New York: New American Library.

Miles, M., & Huberman, M. (1984). *Qualitative data analysis: A sourcebook of new methods*. Beverly Hills, CA: Sage.

Miller, S. (2006). *Conversation: A history of a declining art*. New Haven, CT: Yale University Press.

Mitchell, J. (1984). Typicality and the case study. In R. F. Ellen (Ed.), *Ethnographic research: A guide to conduct* (pp. 238–241). New York: Academic Press.

Nelson, K. (Ed.). (1989). *Narratives from the crib*. Cambridge, MA: Harvard University Press.

New London Group. (1996). A pedagogy of multiliteracies: Designing social futures. *Harvard Educational Review, 66,* 60–92.

Nordstrom, C., & Robben A. (Eds.). (1995). *Fieldwork under fire: Contemporary studies of violence and survival*. Berkeley: University of California Press.

Nunes, T., Schliemann, A., & Caraher, D. (1993). *Street mathematics and school mathematics*. Cambridge, UK: Cambridge University Press.

Ochs, E. (1994). Stories that step into the future. In D. Biber & E. Finegan (Eds.), *Sociolinguistic perspectives on register* (pp. 106–135). Oxford: Oxford University Press.

Ochs, E., & Capps, L. (2001). *Living narrative: Creating lives in everyday storytelling*. Cambridge, MA: Harvard University Press.

Okely, J. (1983). *The traveller gypsies*. Cambridge, UK: Cambridge University Press.

Olson, D. (1977). From utterance to text: The bias of language in speech and writing. *Harvard Educational Review, 47,* 257–281.

Ortner, S. B. (2005). *New Jersey dreaming: Capital, culture and the class of 58* (2nd ed.). Durham, NC: Duke University Press.

Ortner, S. B. (2006). *Anthropology and social theory: Culture, power, and the acting subject*. Durham, NC: Duke University Press.

Pfeifer, R., & Bongard, J. (2007). *How the body shapes the way we think: A new view of intelligence*. Cambridge, MA: MIT Press.

Philips, S. (1972). Participation structures and communicative competence: Warm Springs children in community and classroom. In C. Cazden, V. P. John, & D. H. Hymes (Eds.), *Functions of language in the classroom* (pp. 370–394). New York: Teachers College Press.

Philips, S. (1983). *The invisible culture: Communication in classroom and community on the Warm Springs Indian Reservation*. New York: Longman.

Polanyi, M. (1983). *The tacit dimension*. New York: Doubleday. (Original work published 1966)

Prinsloo, M., & Breier, M. (Eds.). (1996). *Social uses of literacy: Theory and practice in contemporary South Africa*. Amsterdam: John Benjamins.

Ragin, C. C., & Becker, H. S. (1992). *What is a case: Exploring the foundations of social inquiry*. New York: Cambridge University Press.

Rampton, B. (1995). *Crossing: Language and ethnicity among adolescents*. London: Longman Group Limited.

Reyes, A. (2007). *Language, identity and stereotype among Southeast Asian American youth*. Mahwah, NJ: Erlbaum.

Robinson-Pant, A. (Ed.). (2004). *Women, literacy and development: Alternative perspectives*. London: Routledge.

Rogers, A. (Ed.). (2005). *Urban literacy: Communication, identity, and learning in urban contexts*. Hamburg, Germany: UNESCO Institute for Education.

Rogoff, B. (2003). *The cultural nature of human development*. Oxford: Oxford University Press.

Rosaldo, R. (1993). *Culture and truth: The remaking of social analysis*. London: Routledge.

Rose, M. (2004). *The mind at work: Valuing the intelligence of the American worker*. New York: Viking.

Roulleau-Berger, L. (Ed.). (2003). *Youth and work in the post-industrial city of North America and Europe*. Boston: Brill.

Sanjek, R. (Ed.). (1990). *Fieldnotes: The making of anthropology*. Ithaca, NY: Cornell University Press.

Saxe, G. (1988). Candy selling and maths learning. *Educational Researcher, 17*, 14–21.

Schieffelin, B. (1990). *The give and take of everyday life: Language socialization of Kaluli children*. London: Cambridge University Press.

Schieffelin, B., & Ochs, E. (1986). *Language socialization across cultures*. London: Cambridge University Press.

Schiffrin, D. (1988). *Discourse markers*. Cambridge: Cambridge University Press.

Schiffrin, D. (1994). *Approaches to discourse*. Cambridge, UK: Cambridge University Press.

Scribner, S., & Cole, M. (1981). *The psychology of literacy*. Cambridge, MA: Harvard University Press.

Segal, D. A., & Yanagisako, S. J. (Eds.). (2005). *Unwrapping the sacred bundle: Reflections on the disciplining of anthropology*. Durham, NC: Duke University Press.

Sheridan D., Street, B., & Bloome, D. (2000). *Ordinary people writing: Literacy practices and identity in the mass-observation project*. Cresskill, NJ: Hampton.

Shore, C., & Wright, S. (Eds.). (1997). *Anthropology of policy: Critical perspectives on governance and power*. London: Routledge.

Shuman, A. (1986). *Storytelling rights: The uses of oral and written texts by urban adolescents*. Cambridge, UK: Cambridge University Press.

Snow, C., Tabors, P. O., Nicholson, P., & Keuland, B. (1995). SHELL: Oral language and early literacy skills in kindergarten and first grade children. *Journal of Research in Childhood Education, 10*, 37–48.

Spindler, G. (1974). *Education and cultural process: Toward an anthropology of education.* New York: Holt, Rinehart & Winston.

Spindler, G. (1982). *Doing the ethnography of schooling: Educational anthropology in action.* New York: Holt, Rinehart & Winston.

Spindler, G., & Spindler, L. (1970). *Dreamers without power: The Menomini Indians.* New York: Holt, Rinehart & Winston.

Spindler, G., & Spindler, L. (1992). Cultural process and ethnography: An anthropological perspective. In M. D. LeCompte, W. L. Millroy, & J. Preissle (Eds.), *The handbook of qualitative research in education* (pp. 53–91). New York: Academic Press.

Sternberg, R. (1985). *Beyond IQ: A triarchic theory of human intelligence.* Cambridge, UK: Cambridge University Press.

Sternberg, R., & Wagner, R. (1986). *Practical intelligence: Nature and origins of competence in the everyday world.* Cambridge, UK: Cambridge University Press.

Sternberg, R., & Wagner, R. (1994). *Mind in context.* Cambridge, UK: Cambridge University Press.

Stocking, G. (Ed.). (1974). *The shaping of American anthropology, 1883–1911.* New York: Basic Books.

Stocking, G. (1992). *The ethnographer's magic.* Madison: University of Wisconsin Press.

Street, B. (1984). *Literacy in theory and practice.* London: Routledge.

Street, B. (1988). Literacy practices and literacy myths. In R. Saljo (Ed.), *The written world: Studies in literate thought and action* (pp.59–72). Heidelberg, Germany: Springer-Verlag Press.

Street, B. (1993a). (Ed.) *Cross-cultural approaches to literacy.* Cambridge, UK: Cambridge University Press.

Street, B. (1993b). Culture is a verb. In D. Graddol (Ed.), *Language and culture* (pp. 23–43). Clevedon, UK: Multingual Matters/BAAL.

Street, B. (1995). *Social literacies: Critical approaches to literacy in development, education, and ethnography.* London: Longman.

Street, B. (2006). *Understanding and defining literacy.* Scoping paper for EFA global monitoring report. Paris: UNECO.

Street, B., Baker, D., & Tomlin, A. (2005). *Navigating numeracies: Home/school numeracy practices: Vol. 4. Leverhulme Numeracy Research Programme.* Dordrecht, Netherlands: Kleuwen.

Street, B., & Hornberger, N. (Eds.). (2007). *Encyclopedia of language and education: Vol. 2. Literacy.* Hamburg, Germany: Springer.

Sunderland, P., & Denny, R. M. (2007). *Doing anthropology in consumer research.* Walnut Creek, CA: Left Coast Press.

Sunstein, B. S., & Chiseri-Strater, E. (2002). *Fieldworking: Reading and writing research* (2nd ed.). Boston: Bedford/St. Martin's.

Sutton-Smith, B. (1997). *The ambiguity of play.* Cambridge, MA: Harvard University Press.

Tannen, D. (1989). *Talking voices*. Cambridge, UK: Cambridge University Press.

Tannen, D. (1998). *The argument culture*. New York: Balantine.

Thornton, R. (1988). Culture: A contemporary definition. In E. Boonzaeir & J. Sharp (Eds.), *Keywords* (pp. 17–28). Cape Town, South Africa: David Philip.

Todorov. T. (1988). Knowledge in social anthropology: Distancing and universality. *Anthropology Today, 4*(2), 2–5.

Toulmin, S. (1964). *Acts of arguing: A rhetorical model of argument*. Albany: State University of New York Press.

Van Maanen, J. (1988). *Tales of the field: On writing ethnography*. Chicago: University of Chicago Press.

Vincent, D. (1989). *Literacy and popular culture: England, 1750–1914*. Cambridge, UK: Cambridge University Press.

Wagner, D. (1993). *Literacy, culture and development: Becoming literate in Morocco*. Cambridge, UK: Cambridge University Press.

Watt, I. (2001). *The rise of the novel*. Berkeley: University of California Press. (Original work published 1957)

Wax, M. (1971). *Doing fieldwork: Warnings and advice*. Chicago: University of Chicago Press.

Weber, M. (1949). *The methodology of the social sciences*. (E. A. Shils, Trans.). New York: Free Press.

Weir, R. (1962). *Language in the crib*. Berlin: Mouton.

Wenger, E. (1998). *Communities of practice: Learning, meaning and identity*. Cambridge, UK: Cambridge University Press.

Wolcott, H. F. (1967). *A Kwakiutl village and school*. New York: Holt, Rinehart & Winston.

Wolcott, H. (1994). *Transforming qualitative data: Description, analysis and interpretation*. Walnut Creek, CA: Sage.

Wolcott, H. F. (1999). *Ethnography: A way of seeing*. Walnut Creek, CA: Altamira.

Wolcott, H. F. (2001). *The art of fieldwork*. Walnut Creek, CA: Altamira.

Wright, S. (Ed.). (1994). *Anthropology of organizations*. London: Routledge.

Wulff, H. (1998). *Ballet across borders: Career and culture in the world of dancers*. Oxford: Berg.

Zentella, A. (1997). *Growing up bilingual*. London: Blackwell.

Zentella, A. (Ed.). (2005). *Building on strength: Language and literacy in Latino families and communities*. New York: Teachers College Press.

Index

About the Authors

Shirley Brice Heath is Professor at Large in the Watson Institute for International Studies at Brown University; Margery Bailey Professor of English and Dramatic Literature Emerita and Professor of Linguistics Emerita at Stanford University; and Visiting Research Professor in Education at King's College, University of London. Shirley taught for over 20 years at Stanford University in the School of Humanities and Sciences in the departments of English and Linguistics with courtesy appointments in the Anthropology department and the Graduate School of Education. Her fieldwork in the United States, Mexico, Guatemala, South Africa, Australia, and England has centered on local and national language policies and language development from infancy into early adulthood. Of special interest have been underresourced communities and the types of learning environments that children and young people choose and shape for themselves. In particular, she has examined the context of work in the arts and environmental sciences that involves those in middle childhood and adolescence in long-term investigatory projects and community development.

Brian V. Street is Professor of Language in Education at King's College, University of London, and Visiting Professor of Education in both the Graduate School of Education, University of Pennsylvania, and the School of Education and Professional Development, University of East Anglia. Brian undertook anthropological fieldwork on literacy in Iran during the 1970s and taught social and cultural anthropology for over 20 years at the University of Sussex before taking up the Chair of Language in Education at King's College, University of London. He has written and lectured extensively on literacy practices from both a theoretical and an applied perspective. He has a longstanding commitment to linking ethnographic-style research on the cultural dimensions of language and literacy with contemporary practice in education and in development, and he has recently extended this to research on social dimensions of numeracy practices. He has a long-standing involvement with Britain's Mass Observation Project, a historical and contemporary archive of the everyday habits and thoughts of "ordinary people." He has taken part in technical support teams and training programs and research on literacy and numeracy in everyday practice and in schools in the United States, South Africa, Nepal, India, and Iran.